SOLVING
MARRIAGE
PROBLEMS

Resources by Jay E. Adams

The Christian Counselor's Manual
The Christian Counselor's Casebook
Competent to Counsel
Handbook of Church Discipline
How to Help People Change
Marriage, Divorce, and Remarriage in the Bible
Preaching with Purpose
Shepherding God's Flock
Solving Marriage Problems
A Theology of Christian Counseling

SOLVING MARRIAGE PROBLEMS

Biblical Solutions for
Christian Counselors

JAY E. ADAMS

ZONDERVAN™

GRAND RAPIDS, MICHIGAN 49530 USA

ZONDERVAN™

Solving Marriage Problems
Copyright © 1983 by Jay E. Adams

Requests for information should be addressed to:
Zondervan, *Grand Rapids, Michigan 49530*

Library of Congress Cataloging-in-Publication Data

Adams, Jay Edward.
Solving marriage problems.

(The Jay Adams library)
Originally published: Phillipsburg, N.J.:
Presbyterian and Reformed Pub. Co., © 1983.
ISBN 0-310-51081-3
1. Marriage counseling. 2. Pastoral counseling.
3. Marriage—Religious aspects—Christianity.
4. Marriage—Biblical teaching. I. Title. II. Series: Adams, Jay Edward.
Jay Adams library.
BV4012.27.A23   1986   253.5   86-4129

Printed in the United States of America

07 08 / DC / 25 24

To all of those husbands and wives
who truly want to live for Christ,
but don't know how

Contents

Preface

Fifteen years ago, prophets of doom both within the church and without were predicting the end of the marriage institution. With communes, open marriage, and annual, renewable marriage contracts as the current fads, they could see no future for traditional marriage.

In spite of their dire predictions, not only has marriage survived, but Christian marriages are becoming stronger than ever. The attacks on marriage have provoked more preaching and teaching about marriage, more books and conferences on the subject, and more marriage counseling by Bible-believing churches than ever before. That has resulted in a heightened understanding of what marriage is all about, including its purpose and obligations. Christians have come to recognize that they can no longer depend on society to teach the basic principles of marriage and to establish its norms;[1] such instruction must come from the church itself.

1. Not that the church ever should have depended on the schools and the other institutions in our culture to provide these norms, but, of course, it was easy to do so when ostensibly all of society supported the marriage institution.

The church has moved ahead with remarkable speed to explore, to examine, and to exhort. Even a casual survey of the shelves of any Christian book store will indicate how much interest there is in the subject of marriage and the home.

That renewed interest and concern is good. But though the tide against marriage and the family has been turned, all is not well. While Christian counselors work to salvage marriages wrecked under the previous onslaught, new casualties occur as attacks on marriage assume new strategies.

To complicate matters, much of the spate of Christian writing and teaching about marriage has done more harm than good. Strange, unbiblical teachings by well-meaning but ill-informed writers and teachers are beginning to bear their bitter fruit, adding problems within the church to the pressures already felt from without. The harm of which I speak stems often from eclecticism within Christian counseling circles, in which the ideas of the world are accepted, Bible-coated, and then fed to unsuspecting Christians as biblical truths. When these ideas are taught by professors from respected seminaries and Bible colleges, the average Christian assumes that they must have a biblical base.

Given these trends within the church and without, along with the ever-present need for marriage counseling since the original sin in the garden, the counselor who wishes to help Christians in a truly biblical way still has an enormous task ahead of him.

This book is designed to equip him for that task. It is a conscious attempt to avoid all eclecticism, to meet the current attacks from anti-Christian sources, and to correct those dangerous errors that have crept into the church. This book may also serve as a ready reference to which a counselor may turn, especially when the going gets tough.

Moreover, since it covers a wide range of marriage problems, along with the relevant biblical principles and practices, it is also designed to be used as a text for courses in marriage counseling and for general perusal by those who simply wish to sharpen their knowledge and skills regarding marriage.

Teachers who wish to use this text as the basis for a course in marriage counseling will find that I have included assignments at the end of the chapters. These also will be found helpful to students using the book on their own, if they make the necessary alterations in these assignments to apply them to their own situations. Every effort has been made to develop a text that is not only comprehensive but, at the same time, useful and satisfying.[2]

It is my sincere hope that *Solving Marriage Problems* will greatly assist marriage counselors everywhere in their service to Christ's church.

Jay E. Adams
The Millhouse, 1982

---

2. At all points I am presupposing a knowledge of basic, biblical counseling principles as these are found in my four fundamental volumes: *Competent to Counsel* (1970), *The Christian Counselor's Manual* (1973), *Lectures on Counseling* (1977), and *More Than Redemption* (1979), all published by Presbyterian and Reformed Publishing Co., Box 817, Phillipsburg, New Jersey 08865. Parallel readings in these books also may be assigned.

1

Why Marriage Counseling Is So Important

The importance of marriage counseling cannot be doubted. Counselors unanimously find that marriage and family problems outnumber all other counseling problems combined. For that reason alone, counselors should want to learn all they can about marriage counseling.

What's more, marriage itself is first among the institutions created by God and is, therefore, basic to them all. Before government, business, or even the church took institutionalized form, God institutionalized marriage in the Garden of Eden. He Himself set forth its terms, performed the first marriage ceremony, and established marriage as the basic institution of society. Destroy marriage and you destroy the state (as Russia and communist China have been finding out), you destroy business, and you even destroy the church. No wonder the devil has, from the beginning, done all he can to drive his devious wedge between marriage partners.

Because the marriage relationship is so basic, marital counseling is often the catalyst for tremendous individual growth, as each partner learns to handle pressures in the home. When visiting in the Kearney, Nebraska, area some years ago, I was taken for a tour of a valve factory, where we were shown valves of every sort. A memorable part of that tour was the valve-testing procedure. Every valve, no matter what its purpose, size, or shape, was submitted to the same test before being approved for shipment: It was subjected to twice the pressure it would ever have to withstand in actual usage. That pressure brought out any defects that might be present.

The pressures of marriage likewise have a way of bringing out defects. You can't place two sinners—even redeemed ones—under the same roof, at close range, day after day without such pressures. And they are often great enough to expose problems not previously apparent. Although a young couple may consider themselves compatible, they may soon discover the truth that no two sinners are fundamentally compatible. Only as Christ works within the marriage can there be genuine, lasting unity.

It is a myth to assume that compatibility is the sum total of similar likes and dislikes or socio-economic factors in a couple's background. Husbands and wives must grow as individuals in conformity to Christ in order to be compatible with each other. That is why marriage counseling is concerned about individual growth as well as the shared growth of partners.

But perhaps of the greatest importance are two other factors: First, the work of Christ is at stake in marriage counseling. In Ephesians 5, the key section on marriage roles, the relationship between Christ and His church is presented as the norm for marriage.[1] As Christ is to His church, so must a husband be toward his wife; as the church ought to be toward Christ, so must a wife be toward her husband. When a husband and wife approximate the

1. For more on marriage roles, see my book, *Christian Living in the Home* (Phillipsburg, N.J.: Presbyterian and Reformed, 1972).

proper relationship of Christ to His church, they bear a good witness to the saving grace of Christ. When they fail, they bring shame on the name of the Lord.

Second, a couple's relationship to God is sharply affected by their relationship to one another. This important matter, which may impede the prayer lives of more couples than is realized, has been neglected in the teaching of the church. But the Scriptures are explicit:

> Husbands, live with your wives in an understanding way, showing respect for the woman as you would a fragile vase, and as joint heirs of the grace of life, *so that your prayers may not be interrupted* (I Pet. 3:7).

The clause I have placed in italics presents an unmistakable warning. Disharmony in the home is often the chief contributor to disharmony between heaven and the home. That general fact should be made clear in preaching and in marriage counseling. No counseling can proceed effectively apart from the willingness of both parties (though in the passage quoted the husband is especially singled out) to confess sin, be reconciled to one another, and do whatever they discover God requires of them in counseling. Apart from that, counseling cannot proceed because prayers for its success will not be heard. Many other problems in marriages will never be settled, problems with finances, or children, for example, until there is harmony between husband and wife. Communication with God is at stake. When a husband refuses to communicate with his wife, he can be assured on the basis of I Peter 3:7 that God will refuse to hear his communications.

We have seen something of the importance of marriage counseling. Though much else could be said, I have chosen to focus on its essential nature. It will be important, as we go along, to keep in mind the specific scope of this book.

First, what this book is *not* about:

1. Marriage, not the family, is our concern. The home,

including counseling problems regarding discipline and child rearing, demands a separate treatment. We shall consider children and in-laws only as they become a factor in the relationship of spouses to one another.

2. Marriage, not divorce and remarriage, is the focus of this book. Because I have written extensively about divorce and remarriage elsewhere, there is no need to duplicate that work here.[2]

3. Marriage, not premarital counseling, is the issue here. Premarital counseling is important, and I have written about it in *Shepherding God's Flock*.[3] For the most extensive study of the subject, see Howard Eyrich's book, *Three to Get Ready*.[4]

4. Marriage problems, not preventive counseling, are in view. Again, that subject is crucial and deserves separate, full treatment. However, many of the principles found in this volume, turned inside out, provide help for preventive counseling as well.

5. Marriage, not sex within marriage, is the subject of this book. Of course, something must be said about sex, but, once more, the complete consideration that important issue deserves belongs to a separate book.

Second, what this book *is* about:

1. Marriage problems—of all sorts. The principal problems that counselors face in the day-to-day work of counseling will be covered. Inclusion in this book will indicate that a problem is of frequent occurrence.

2. Causes of these problems. While Adam's sin is the ultimate cause of every problem, including all marriage problems, the Bible itself does not merely point

2. See *Marriage, Divorce and Remarriage in the Bible* (Phillipsburg, N.J.: Presbyterian and Reformed, 1980).

3. One-volume edition (Phillipsburg, N.J.: Presbyterian and Reformed, 1980), pp. 234-53.

4. Phillipsburg, N.J.: Presbyterian and Reformed, 1978.

out that fact and leave it there; it goes on to discuss the proximate causes as well. Because this is a biblical pattern, we shall do the same.

3. Ways of detecting, categorizing, naming, and describing problems in a biblical manner.

4. Ways of reaching biblical solutions to marriage problems.

Knowing something about why marriage counseling is important and the scope of this book, you will be able to *concentrate* your efforts on this *all-important* area. As you begin, make it your goal to learn all that you can. If you do, you will be far better prepared to help the hundreds of people around you who desperately need biblical guidance and direction in their marriages. As you work diligently toward that goal, my prayer is that you will find this book of invaluable assistance.

Assignment

Make a list of all of the marriage problems you have encountered, either in your own family or in the families of those who are well known to you. Define and describe each problem and note whether it was solved biblically or not. Also, place question marks beside any of these problems to which you do not already know the biblical solution.

From among those problems you and others have marked with a question mark, compose a list of problems for the whole class to consider. As each problem is taken up in the book, bring out the problem on the list, describe it in some detail (but flatten out the details so that no one would know whom you are talking about), and discover how the principles discussed in the book apply to it. The teacher and a secretary, chosen from the class (whose duty it is to alert the class to the problem at the appropriate time) should each receive a copy of the list. In small classes, every member may be given a photocopied list.

2

The Counselor's Own Marriage

There are Christian counselors who are ineffective not because of unbiblical motives or an unacquaintance with the biblical principles and practices for marriage counseling, but simply because their own marriages are a mess. Their prayers for their counselees are interrupted. How can they help others when they are unwilling to be helped themselves?

Such counselors, when faced with the marital problems of others, cannot with conviction and power urge the biblical solutions they themselves refuse to practice. Blinded by their own sin to the importance of a biblical truth or practice, how can they discover and apply it to others?

When you hear some of the advice given to couples having marital difficulties, you understand why they have not been helped, and you understand why preachers and Christian workers who offer such advice are so powerless in their ministries. If they themselves do the same things they urge on their counselees, no wonder their own marriages go astray. No wonder their counseling is so weak and ineffective!

When you hear of a preacher advising a young couple not to have anything to do with troublesome, unconverted in-laws, for instance, instead of urging them to follow Romans 12:18 ("If possible, so far as it depends on you, be at peace with everybody"—in-laws included),[1] you have to wonder what his relationship to his own in-laws must be like. When you learn that another preacher allows one spouse to keep privileged information away from the other, rather than insisting that such information be shared in order to preserve open communication along with "one-flesh" closeness and coordination in the marriage,[2] again you wonder how much closeness or coordination there is between that preacher and his wife.

What I am saying is that not only is it necessary to acquire proper principles of counseling and be aware of how biblically to use them but, even more so a counselor must develop and maintain a marriage that itself is holy and flourishing according to biblical standards. You must not ignore in your own marriage what you advise for others. Otherwise, you will lack the insight and power to help others, which comes from none other than the Holy Spirit. God nowhere promises to bless hypocrites.

Who then is equal to the task? Who is qualified to counsel? Whose marriage properly exemplifies the relationship of Christ to His church and the church to Christ?

Those are important questions. They are not meant to entangle counselors in paralyzing doubt or deter them from counseling altogether. The Bible sets forth no unrealistic standards. Take, for instance, the standards for an elder. While they prohibit laying hands on unqualified men, they are not so strict that no one is able to fill the office (I Tim. 3; Titus 1). Similarly, while it is important for Christian coun-

1. See also the many other pertinent verses in Rom. 12:13-21.
2. See Eph. 4:25: "each one must speak the truth with his neighbor, since we are members of one another."

selors to counsel under the assurance that their own marriages count for Christ, that does not mean their marriages must be perfect. If perfection were essential, no one would be qualified to counsel, preach, or for that matter, do anything for Christ. No, something short of perfection is required; yet, on the other hand, something short of hypocrisy and failure in one's own marriage is prerequisite.

How shall we find the proper biblical place between these extremes?

First of all, let me warn against those blind guides of the blind who think their shipwrecked marriages qualify them to help others. Too many who have failed miserably, even to the point of divorce, regard themselves as expert marriage counselors because of their firsthand absorption in marital problems. "I've been through it all," they tell themselves, "so I can share out of my experience." It is not experience, but biblical truth and skills developed by biblical principles that qualify someone to counsel. Not even the experience of a *successful* marriage is enough. True, there may be cases in which, by God's good grace, some have magnificently turned horrible failures into sterling successes, as God assures us that "where sin abounded, grace far more abounded" (Rom. 5:20); but in those cases the change in the person's lifestyle is so great that it is obvious a dramatic work of God's grace has occurred. It is also apparent not only that he has dealt with all of his past failures in a completely biblical manner, but that his marriage now exemplifies Christ's relationship to His church. And it is equally clear that he intends to counsel not out of his experience, but out of the revealed Word of God.[3]

It seems there is no end of self-appointed marriage counselors in the church. It is time for the church to discourage

3. For more on the proper place and use of experience, see my book, *Grist from Adams's Mill* (Phillipsburg, N.J.: Presbyterian and Reformed, 1983).

the blind from misguiding the blind. Too many marriages have ended in the ditch because their advice was followed.

The balance we are seeking will be found when the following two conditions are met: (1) The counselor must not wait until his marriage is perfect before counseling others; otherwise, he'll never begin. (2) A counselor may help others when his own marriage is an example to others. (That is what also qualifies the pastor to speak: Titus 2:7 requires him to be an example "in all things.") To be an example, as many biblical passages imply, is possible without perfection. One way the counselor can be an example is by handling his failures biblically, as well as following other biblical requirements.

A counselor must constantly care and repair, if he is to be an example. If married, he must be a person whose marriage is moving in the right direction, solving problems in a thoroughly biblical fashion. In short, a counselor must be able to say with David, "I walk . . . with integrity in my house" (Ps. 101:2ᵇ). The word *tam*, which is translated "integrity," means "having it all together." Unless a counselor is in the process of getting it all together, willing and determined to have it all together, and resolving any difficulties that keep him from doing so, he is unable to counsel others.

3
What Causes Marriage Problems?

Types of Causes

In this and the following chapters I shall discuss some of the proximate causes of marriage problems. Obviously, the basic cause is always sin. But sin manifests itself in two ways: in erroneous concepts and in sinful attitudes or practices. In all cases error must be replaced by truth, and sinful practices must be replaced by a new lifestyle that is pleasing to God. Often evil practices grow out of erroneous ideas, though not always.

The Bible distinguishes between particular sinful practice and errors, and it exposes and corrects both (see II Tim. 3:16, 17); it does not simply lump them all under the heading of "sin" or "Adam's sin" and leave it at that. Granted it is sin to believe, teach, and live according to error, even when one does not recognize it as error, just as it is to live in ways that one knows to be sin. And, surely, both recognized and unrecognized sinful thinking and living patterns are the result of one's sinful nature inherited from Adam.

But we must also recognize, as the Bible does, the more intimate or proximate causes of marriage failure, along with their ultimate cause.

How important is it to identify these more immediate causes? For one thing, when ideas are found to be in error, they may be corrected from the Word of God. Exhortations to live right will do no good until one has a clear idea of what is expected. Wrong living will be changed only by rooting out the fundamental cause in a person's thinking.

In other cases, where someone knows the right way and understands the biblical truth, but refuses to live by that truth, that unwillingness must be spotted and confronted. It will do little good in such cases to instruct the guilty party again in what he already understands. Here is where proper biblical exhortation is precisely what is needed.

Then again, if someone unwittingly brings into his marriage sinful living patterns, which begin to cause problems, and recognizing their sinfulness, he is willing to repent and change, but does not know how to replace them with biblical living patterns, that calls for a third approach: help in replacing sinful habits with righteous ones. In short, each proximate cause—wrong thinking, wrong living persisted in, and wrong living due to habits difficult to replace —leads to a different approach from the counselor.

Sinful versus Nonsinful Causes

In order to identify the cause of a problem, we need to decide whether the problem is an error, a wilful sin, or a failure to overcome a pattern. In doing so, we must recognize that if the Bible calls a given practice a "sin," it is wrong to call it anything else. For instance, to call sin "sickness" or "immaturity," or to use any of the other psychological or sociological jargon that distorts or disguises its true nature, is to lead yourself and your counselee astray.

Words, the semanticists tell us, are signs of the things they signify. But that's not all. They are also sign*posts*. Label a sinful action or practice a "sickness," and you have altered the situation significantly. To call homosexual behavior "sickness," for instance, when the Bible calls it an "abomination" and "something worthy of death" is to point the homosexual in the direction of a physician for the solution to his problem. To call it "sin" is to point him to Jesus Christ. Labels, you see, are signposts, not merely signs; they point in the direction of a solution. Therefore, it is very important to give marriage problems either biblical or biblically derived labels. Other labels tell lies about problems and inevitably point to the wrong solutions.

When identifying causes of marriage problems, it is just as important to call a true sickness (e.g., a brain tumor that is adversely affecting one spouse's behavior) "sickness" as it is to call sin "sin." Biblical counselors are not interested in gumming the label "sin" on everything in sight, as some wrongly and carelessly accuse us of doing. No, it is just because we wish to be responsible before God and man that we use the label "sin" when it is biblically appropriate. And it is for the same reason that we use other labels when they are accurate. Our zeal for ripping off modern labels and replacing them with "sin" is due to persistent efforts by others to substitute some modern misleading term for that biblical label. The new jargon is usually a sampling of a "psychological" system totally out of accord with scriptural principles.

Those who busily replace the word "sin" with modern labels may think they are kind in doing so. Calling drunkenness a "disease" or a "sickness" rather than a "sin" may seem to them to be a gracious act, but it is just the opposite. You cannot be more gracious than God. To call drunkenness a "sickness" is to take away hope; there is no pill that will cure such a "disease." But if, as the Bible says, drunkenness is a sin, then there is real hope, because Christ Jesus came not only to free us from the penalty but also from the power of sin. Drunkenness is included in the list of sins in I Corinthians 6:9-11, from which Paul assured the Corinthians they had been delivered (v. 11). When Alcoholics Anonymous tells someone he will have to remind himself every day for the rest of his life that he is an alcoholic, is that kinder than the Bible? Paul assures homosexuals and drunkards that "these are what some of you *were.*" You *can* get beyond being a drunkard, Paul says.

The difference in labeling leads to a difference in thinking about the problem, which, in turn, leads to a different solution and ultimately to a different outcome. What begins by sounding kind ends up destroying hope.

Likewise, if a marriage is disturbed by the selfishness of one spouse, it is wrong to call that selfishness "immaturity." That may sound milder and kinder, but is it? No. What can you do about immaturity? Nothing but set up the conditions for growth. And you must wait for the growth. But if the problem is identified as "selfishness," something can be done right away: The one sinning may repent and begin to show love to his or her spouse by pursuing the commands found in Philippians 2:3, 4. Is it kinder to say to the one who is abused, "Well, you'll just have to wait until your spouse grows up," or to say to the offender, "This sinful way of life can be changed if you will confess it as sin and adopt God's new ways instead. If you're willing, I'll help you, and you can start making changes today"?

This book is devoted to an approach that is genuinely kind: calling sin "sin." When, however, there may be an organic reason for any problem, the counselor should always advise the counselee to have a thorough medical evaluation. The *Journal of Pastoral Practice* (published and distributed by the Christian Counseling and Educational

Foundation, 1790 E. Willow Grove Ave., Laverock, Pennsylvania 19118) has for years been running articles on various medical problems that influence behavior and attitudes, in order to familiarize biblical counselors with signs and symptoms that indicate the need for a medical checkup. Because organic problems, which result from Adam's sin and the subsequent curse, are not in themselves sin, Christian counselors must become thoroughly acquainted with their symptoms and advise counselees accordingly.

To put it simply, biblical counselors wish to be accurate. They want to call what is truly sin "sin" and what is truly sickness "sickness." Any other determination leads to more and greater difficulties. Problems are misidentified, complicated, and prolonged. In the absence of a biblically accurate description of problems, the road to their solutions is cut off.

Identifying Complicating Problems

So, counselor, think seriously about the causes of marriage problems. Causes are often complex. Usually, complicating problems arise. For instance, suppose there is an organic difficulty, undetected. And suppose bad attitudes have developed because of this problem. And further, suppose communication has broken down. Now, the organic difficulty is discovered and treated. Will all be well? No. Even if the organic difficulty is corrected and the symptoms clear up, the attitudes and the patterns that developed around it will remain unless the counselor deals with them. Complicating problems like these will remain unidentified unless the counselor suspects their presence and probes for them.

Suppose the organic problem cannot be corrected. Again, not only will the counselor find it necessary to help

the couple eliminate sinful attitudes and patterns they have
developed over the months or years, but he will also have to
help them to replace these with new patterns and attitudes,
including a Christian outlook on the organic difficulty, and
ways of dealing with it biblically.

In the next few chapters I shall deal specifically with
many of the nonorganic problems that destroy marriages.
Counselors must know these proximate causes and be prepared at all times to deal with them in a biblical fashion.
They are of two sorts, as I have already pointed out: problems of error, stemming from the noetic effects of sin, and
problems of practice.[1] The former we shall consider under
the heading of "Unbiblical Concepts of Marriage," and the
latter, under "Sinful Living Patterns." While two additional
factors might be assumed under either of these two head-
ings, they are of such importance that I shall consider them
separately under the titles "Relationships with Others" and
"General Influences in Society." These four areas will provide you with many items that can be used as a check list for
discovering what, in any given case, is the cause (or causes)
of marital difficulty.

Assignment

After individuals or groups study different issues of the
Journal of Pastoral Practice, have each individual or group
present an oral report to the entire class. Each report must
describe some organic difficulty mentioned in the *Journal*,
together with its signs and symptoms. The report might
also suggest ways of dealing with the complicating counseling problems that often grow out of each organic difficulty.

List as many instances as you can of how error may lead
to conflict and other difficulties in marriage. Describe an
actual situation or two out of your past experience in which

1. I subsume problems of attitude under this heading.

you have known that to happen. Be sure to flatten out the case so that it would be impossible for anyone else to tell whom you are talking about.

Begin thinking about what sorts of patterns a single person might develop that would become a problem in a marriage. Jot down your thoughts for use later on in class discussion.

Compile a list of modern labels that wrongly identify problems. Alongside each of these place the correct biblical label or labels.

4

Unbiblical Concepts of Marriage: Central Errors

While any error may and does cause difficulty in marriage, here I wish to limit my discussion to erroneous views of marriage, which lead to wrong expectations, attitudes, and practices. It is here, sad to say, that many Christians—even Bible-believing Christians—go wrong. Their concept of marriage is an illusion. For that reason, we must spend some time discussing the nature of marriage.

The Origin of Marriage

Most Christians understand the origin of marriage, although many are unaware of the significance of that origin. Let me set forth the basic tenet that must be affirmed and then consider its practical relevance to marital life. First, and foremost, a Christian must clearly understand that *marriage is of divine origin*. That might sound like a truism, except for the fact that everywhere today we are being told otherwise. In colleges and high schools, our young people are taught that marriage came about not by divine fiat but as a humanly devised expedient. Those two viewpoints are not only antithetical, but lead to widely differing consequences in marriage.

If marriage is a divinely ordained institution, as the Bible purports, then it should persist until God ordains otherwise; the rules and ideals of marriage are to be those which He set forth; and marriage must not be revamped by human whim or expediency. If, on the other hand, marriage came about as a human expedient, devised by man, and all of its terms were of human origin, then it certainly may be abolished or its terms may be altered by man for whatever reasons he wishes.

Young people in our churches do not have a strong idea of the divine origin of marriage. The church has naively assumed that they understand this teaching and has not adequately taught them the biblical facts. The home has been equally deficient. How will young people learn? Not from the propaganda they read and hear in the media or in school. There they will be told just the opposite. If they are constantly bombarded with the message that marriage is but a human expedient, they will eventually believe it and, holding to this low view of marriage, will act accordingly. That means that biblical terms for marriage will tend to strike them as irrelevant or at best an optional viewpoint. It means that they will build their marriages out of wrong materials and will aim for something far beneath biblical standards.

Because of the prevailing situation, counselors should find out their counselees' concepts of the origin of marriage. It is senseless and fruitless to presuppose that counselees grasp the biblical view of marriage. That presumption is doomed to failure. It is essential to ascertain the facts before going very far. More often than you may think, one spouse or both fail to understand the origin of marriage and what that fact implies. When a counselor discovers a weak view of the origin of marriage and the implications of its divine ordination, he must take the time to present the biblical view, usually over against the faulty views of marriage-as-a-human-expedient, so widely held today.

The Purpose of Marriage

More frequent, and of even greater consequence, is the failure of Christians to understand the essence of marriage itself. We hear, even in truly Christian circles, some of the strangest ideas about what the purpose of marriage is supposed to be. Unless both spouses understand and set their hearts upon realizing the true purpose of marriage, their marriage will fall far short of what it should be.

What is the purpose of marriage? What, after all else is stripped away, can be said to be its essence? The answer to that question is set forth by God Himself in Genesis 2:18:

> The Lord God said: It is not good for the man to be alone. . . .

The purpose of marriage is to meet man's need for companionship. Marriage was designed to defeat loneliness. Companionship is, therefore, the essence of marriage. This same stress on companionship is found elsewhere. Consider:

> . . . the strange woman . . . who forsakes the companion of her youth and forgets the covenant of her God (Prov. 2:16a, 17);

and

> . . . the Lord has been witness between you and the wife of your youth, to whom you have been faithless, although she is your companion and your wife by covenant (Mal. 2:14).

In these verses, companionship is closely associated with

marriage. Aloneness can be countered only by means of the two elements found in the two distinct words translated "companion" in Proverbs and Malachi. Each of the two words refers to one side of companionship. The word used in Proverbs refers to one "in intimate relationship with"; the word in Malachi refers to one "associated with, or united to." Together, they speak of a relationship in which there is constant commitment and intimacy. Intimacy apart from commitment to remain together is not adequate; commitment to remain in association apart from intimacy is equally deficient. Both elements are necessary to defeat loneliness.

Many wrong ideas about the purpose of marriage are afloat. Perhaps the most common is the belief that marriage is primarily for the propagation of the human race. That belief confuses mating and marriage. The human race, like gerbils, or cats, or rats, does not need the marriage institution for that purpose. Indeed, in many places, the human race, like animal races, is being propagated all too successfully without the benefits of marriage!

No, marriage is more than mating. Marriage is companionship, one aspect of which involves mating. The intimacy of biblical companionship extends to every aspect of human nature. That is one reason why sexual relations are to be limited to the marriage relationship. There can be no intimate companionship between two persons when a third intervenes. Fornication, adultery, and even polygamy vitiate true companionship because they destroy the intimacy of a constant, close relationship. There is an exclusiveness to this "one flesh" relationship (which I shall discuss later).

Most persons who enter marriage with the belief that marriage is simply legitimized sex also have a grossly unbiblical idea of the next important concept that we must explore:

The Obligation of Marriage

You may wonder why I speak of the *obligation* of marriage —in the singular—when, of course, there are many obligations (for instance, Paul speaks in I Cor. 7 of the obligation of sexual relations). When I speak of the obligation of marriage, I have in mind the basic obligation underlying all others (including the sexual obligation). That basic obligation is to meet the other's need for companionship. When a couple takes marriage vows, whether they realize it or not (and often they do not), they are vowing to provide companionship for one another for the rest of their lives; that is what their vows amount to. Notice, they do not vow to receive companionship, but to provide it for one another. Marriage itself is an act of love in which one person vows to meet another's need for life, no strings attached.

That means that when a husband or a wife complains, "I am not getting what I want out of marriage," his or her statement is nonsensical. And you must reply, "You did not enter marriage in order to get something for yourself. You vowed to give something to your partner. Marriage is not a bargain in which each partner says, 'I will give so much in return for so much.' Each vows to give all that is necessary to meet his or her spouse's need for companionship, whether or not he or she receives anything in return. Therefore, the only question for you is, 'Are you fulfilling your vows?' " Many marry for what they can get out of the marriage; but that is lust, not love, and is biblically untenable. For that reason it is often necessary to challenge counselees about their inadequate views of marriage and their failures to live up to their stated vows. As an act of love, marriage vows commit one to giving, not getting.[1] Therefore, the Christian counselor must help his counselees see that the fundamental question is, "How can I please God

1. For more on this, see *Competent to Counsel.*

and my mate?" not "How can I please myself?" To please God by rightly pleasing one's spouse is the basic obligation of marriage.

That basic obligation is foremost, for instance, when discussing priorities in marriage, when struggling with sexual issues, and when making many decisions between matters of preference.[2] The marriage counselor must, therefore, tuck it in the back of his mind. He will find himself reverting to it time and again. It is the sobering truth needed to end many complaints. Get a good grasp on its meaning and learn how to use it effectively; it is a weapon in marriage counseling without parallel.

I have already hinted that there is still a good bit more to obtaining a firm understanding of marriage. In my previous remarks, I spoke of commitment. This leads us to the next important concept.

The Commitment of Marriage

Marriage without commitment is a sorry situation. When a marriage may at any time be brought to an end by either partner, it doesn't have a chance. As things go wrong, which they will in any agreement between sinners,[3] there is little hope if there is no commitment to resolving the problems. With no obligation to do so, many do not; they just call it quits.

The Bible describes marriage as a "covenant," the word for the most solemn and most binding agreement known to

---

2. For a full discussion of decision making in questions of preference, see *More than Redemption*.

3. There is more than enough struggle in an agreement between two parties, when only *one* of which is a sinner, as the broken covenants between God and man make clear.

mankind. There is commitment in marriage; it is a *covenant of companionship.*[4]

Marriage involves a covenantal agreement to meet all of your spouse's needs for companionship (on every level: sexual, social, spiritual, etc.) for the rest of your life. It is, therefore, a final act. Christians, unlike non-Christians today who enter into trial marriages, annual, renewable marriage contracts, and the like, need not live daily under the threat of divorce. The binding nature of the divine covenant assures them that divorce is not an option. That is a wonderful difference that Christians possess. The covenant is a life commitment.

How do we know that marriage is a covenantal commitment? In the two passages quoted above, from Proverbs and from Malachi, it is called a covenant. To them may be added Ezekiel 16:8[b]:

> I plighted My troth to you and entered into a covenant with you, says the Lord God, and you became Mine (Berkeley).

In Malachi, God says that husbands and wives become one "by covenant"; in Ezekiel, we catch that process in the act. The "covenant" of one's "youth," to which both Proverbs and Malachi refer, is the marriage covenant, as the Hebrew parallelism makes clear.[5] Plainly God considers marriage a life commitment of the most solemn sort.[6]

What do I mean by describing a covenant as an ageement

---

4. The phrase *covenant of companionship* should be taught to all counselees. It summarizes the whole of biblical marriage in a memorable way. Make them learn it so that they can tell you, and later remind each other, what marriage is all about. Of course, they will find the phrase itself empty unless you have previously filled it with content for them.

5. Incidentally, in those two passages, both the husband and the wife are called their spouses' companions, indicating that both need companionship, not the man alone, and that both entered into a covenant of companionship before God.

6. That the marriage commitment is for life is clear from Romans 7:2.

of the most solemn and binding sort? Perhaps the best way to get to the heart of that is to refer to the incident recorded in Genesis 15:8-21, in which God entered into covenant with Abraham. There we read that animals were cut into halves (v. 10), which were laid opposite each other. Then, when the sun had set and a dense darkness had fallen (v. 17), there appeared a burning torch (signifying the presence of God), which passed between the pieces.

But what was that all about? When a covenant was made, as the Hebrew clearly indicates, it was "cut." One does not *make* a covenant but, literally, "cuts a covenant." That wording refers to the act described in Genesis 15. Because a covenant was so solemn, it was accompanied by the death of animals, which were *cut* in two. By that act, one declared that he would keep his promises under the pain of death. He said that if he failed to live up to his covenant promises, he was willing to be cut in pieces! God, in covenanting with Abraham, took upon Himself the curse of the covenant, declaring by His act, "May I be torn apart if I do not fulfil my covenant obligations to you." It was a bold figure, implying the most fearful consequences for failing to keep one's oath. That is why I say that marriage is a solemn commitment, binding on those who enter into it.

Most counselees have had inadequate instruction about most of what I am writing. It is the task of the counselor to inform and warn them. God considers their entrance into a marriage covenant from His perspective, whether they did or not, just as He held those Israelites who entered into covenant with Him responsible for keeping its terms, whether they understood and meant it or not.

In this chapter I have begun to discuss some of the fundamental misconceptions of marriage that counselors encounter. They themselves must first comprehend the biblical concepts that have been discussed, before they can help others do so. It is, therefore, of great importance for each counselor to learn them thoroughly and to be able to teach them and reason from them. Do not leave this chapter until you have mastered its contents. What you find here will be fundamental to all you do.

Assignment

Each student should take one concept taught in this chapter and use it in dealing with a case (real or fictitious; again, if real, flatten out the details) in which a faulty concept of marriage is causing difficulty in a marriage. Write the case out or have it prepared to present to the class for discussion, as the instructor directs.

5

Unbiblical Concepts of Marriage: Related Errors

There are any number of other errors that cause trouble within marriages. In this chapter, however, I shall confine my discussion to three of them: (1) a wrong idea of love, (2) the notion that things can be much the same after marriage as before, and (3) the view that mixed marriages don't make any difference. All three of these widely held concepts have brought havoc to marriages, and every biblical counselor must be well prepared to deal with them.

A Wrong Idea of Love

There is a widespread notion that romantic love is necessary to form a strong, biblical marriage. While nothing that I say must be understood to denigrate the idea of romantic love itself as pursued biblically (surely Jacob's love for Rachel is exemplary), nevertheless, the idea that such love is a ground for marriage is unbiblical.

That last statement would probably be unintelligible to most Americans (even Christians) or sound like the rankest

heresy! Yet, it is altogether true. The Bible nowhere makes
romantic love a ground or basis for marriage. In fact, like
most of the marriages in the history of mankind, it allows
for marriages made by the family. Indeed, in other lands
and cultures, after settling on the proper dowry, other
members of the family often have determined who will be
married to whom. Often the first time a husband sees his
bride is when he lifts the veil on the wedding night. Yet,
even under those conditions, two Christians, who love God
and are willing to solve all problems according to His Word,
can make a success of marriage. As a matter of fact, marriages based on romantic love, common to American culture and throughout the West, evidence far less stability
than those not based on romantic love. So, before criticiz-
ing, we should look more carefully at the record.

"But, I thought love is considered an essential part of
marriage. And didn't you say that the act of commitment in
the wedding vows is an act of unconditional love?" Yes,
both comments are true. But you must distinguish carefully
between two things: (1) love as the ground and basis for
marriage and (2) love as an obligation and privilege of
marriage. Although "romantic love" (romantic feelings toward another) is not a condition necessary to the *making* of a
marriage, acts of love toward one's spouse become a permanent obligation from the very moment of covenantal
commitment. This love, which is an essential part of the
marriage contract, is deeper than romantic love and involves the giving of one's self toward another. As I have
shown elsewhere, however, when one gives himself to
another, feelings of love follow acts of love.[1] So, while
feelings of love are not essential for establishing a marriage
contract, they are an inevitable result of properly pursuing
its terms.

The whole notion of love-as-feeling is one that counselors

1. The subject is discussed at length in *Competent to Counsel*, pp. 249f.

must understand and deal with. The love required of us is not something we feel (a love not under voluntary control), but something we show (a love under our control, commanded in the Bible). The first is self-oriented;[2] the second is other-oriented. The model for married love, according to Ephesians 5:25, is God's love for His church. God did not become enamored with the human race, but He did love men, in spite of their sin, by sending His Son to die for them. It is not because we were so lovable, so lovely, or so loving that God loved us; rather, He loved us "while we were enemies." There was nothing in us to attract Him. God simply determined, out of His own good will, to *set* His love on us.[3]

We read, "God so loved the world that He *gave* . . ."; "He loved us and *gave* Himself up for us . . ."; "Love your enemies . . ."; ". . . if your enemy hungers [or] thirsts, *give*. . . ." Love in the Bible begins with giving. Love is the giving of yourself for another; it is giving your time, your interest, your thought, your consideration, your money, your creativity, or even your very life. When one regularly gives himself to another, he deposits a "treasure" in that other person, and that is where his "heart will be also." (In the Bible, the heart is the entire inner person—thoughts as well as feelings.) This basic, self-giving, self-initiated love is the love required in marriage, and it is the very love that will make any Christian marriage a success.

Even if two persons have married for all the wrong reasons, even if they have made a deplorable failure of their marriage for years, there is still great hope for them to

2. Self-oriented pursuits are both sinful and fruitless. True and lasting feelings of love, like happiness, joy, peace, etc., are the by-product of other-oriented activity. To seek self-fulfillment in marriage is wrong. Love in marriage means, first, to seek the welfare and fulfillment of one's spouse.

3. That is why husbands and wives who have strong negative feelings toward one another can learn to love each other in spite of those feelings.

transform that marriage into one that sings—if they repent and are now willing to begin loving each other God's way with God's help. Following repentance, consisting of the confession of sins to God and one another, they must be taught how to demonstrate love in the marriage. That also is where the counselor must help. He usually will need to work with them over a period of time to make sure they implement biblical principles correctly and faithfully.

In the unbiblical model, love just happens; one is passive. He is required to do nothing. There is no time, effort, sacrifice, or learning involved. It is just the opposite of true, giving love. Such love cost God His Son. It will cost a husband and wife too. They will have to nurture and cultivate love for it to grow. But that is part of what the marriage vow is all about. The minister does not ask the bride and groom, "*Do* you love him/her?" but, "*Will* you love . . . ?" Marriage is not based on an existing emotion, but on the promise that one will give love to his or her spouse throughout their lives together.

Young people today talk about pursuing relationships with one another. Such talk is poorly conceived. Relationships do not develop in a vacuum. They form as friendships, when people do other things together. And they develop through deep sharing of thoughts and concerns, which, *par excellence*, typifies the intimacy of marriage. In the greatest passage on friendship ever written, Jesus drew a distinction between the friend and the slave:

> I call you slaves no longer, because the slave doesn't know what his lord is doing. But I have called you friends, because I have made known to you everything that I heard from My Father (John 15:15).

What distinguishes a friendship from other personal contacts is the depth of sharing involved. Friendship is built on a willingness of people to disclose their innermost concerns.

Husbands and wives should be the closest of all friends. Above all other relationships, marriage requires a willingness to cultivate self-disclosure.

When a husband asks, "Do I have to tell my wife that I committed adultery now that I have repented, broken off the affair, and received God's forgiveness?," he must be reminded of the "one flesh" relationship in marriage. God designed a closeness of husband and wife so intimate, so strong, so intertwined in all dimensions, that nothing—not even clothing—should come between. When Genesis tells us that Adam and Even were naked and "unashamed," the issue was not shame over sexual organs. Rather they were so united that they had nothing to hide; their relationship was one of utter frankness. They were entirely open to one another.

When sin came into the picture, they covered themselves and began to hide. Clothing is the symbol of this broken intimacy between them and between them and God. To strip naked before one's spouse is to become open and vulnerable again (cf. Heb. 4:13, where nakedness and vulnerability are joined).

While becoming "one flesh" includes the sexual relationship, that is not its primary meaning. Later in Genesis, when God speaks of destroying "all flesh" in the flood, He is referring to "everybody." The emphasis of our word "everybody" is not every *body*, but every *person*. Similarly, the Hebrew word for "flesh" means "person." That is why in Joel 2, predicting the outpouring of the Holy Spirit, Joel said that the Spirit would be poured on "all flesh." It was not the flesh as opposed to bones that he had in mind, but all kinds of persons—young, old, male, female, as he goes on to say in the context.

So, when Moses writes that the "two shall become one flesh," he means that the intimacy of marriage is so great that it is like two persons becoming one person. That is how

Paul uses the verse from Genesis 2, which he quotes in Ephesians 5. There he says that what the husband does for his wife, he also does for himself—because they have become one person.

For that reason an extramarital affair, so destructive to the unity-in-intimacy of marriage, always disrupts the "one flesh" relationship. If the husband says, "But she doesn't know," he may be right on one level, but certainly not on another. She may not know that he has had an affair, but she will know that something is wrong in their relationship. Indeed, she may even think she's done something to cause the break. Either way, interruption of intimacy and closeness in marriage is a sin against the wife and must be confessed to her.

Things Are Still the Same

Another misconception relates directly to what I have been saying. When two persons merge into one and "cleave" to each other (the Hebrew means to adhere, or be glued together), their marriage constitutes a situation so radically new that neither party can be the same as before. Marriage brings about definite and substantial change in both parties, or at least it should. And it will if the marriage is properly pursued.

But some people don't see it that way. They say, "Things will not be all that different. I can still go about doing the same things that I did before marriage—fishing, bowling with the boys, whatever I please." Wrong. One's priorities must change radically with marriage. A husband must put his wife first, before any other person, and consider her interests of greater moment than his own. Contrary to the feminist emphasis, a wife may not pursue a career as if she were not truly married; rather, she must become husband-oriented in all that she does, including any work she does outside the home.[4] The modern idea that a husband and wife must each live as a person in his or her own right is contrary to the biblical emphasis. The husband is to give himself for his wife in love as Christ did for the church, and the wife is to submit herself to the husband as the church is to submit to Christ. In the pursuit of this twofold effort, which I shall discuss in more detail at a later point, the "one-flesh" relationship develops—and in no other way.

People seek intimacy with others in group therapy, in human potential programs, at Esalen, and elsewhere, but it is found only within the covenant of companionship, where there are commitment for life, willingness to do God's will, and two persons striving by God's help, in Christ, to recover the "one-flesh" relationship Adam and Eve lost. *Marriage is a commitment to become a new person.* The counselor must keep this in mind and be ready to address ideas contrary to the biblical teaching. He may otherwise miss important clues that would alert him to serious misconceptions along these lines.

Mixed Marriages Don't Make Any Difference

When Paul commands believers to marry "only in the Lord" (I Cor. 7:39), he prohibits marriages with unbelievers. Whatever may be the exact import of the phrase "in the Lord," it obviously means, at the very least, within the sphere of relationship to the Lord that one has in salvation. In Scripture, especially in Paul, one's relationship "in Christ" and "in the Lord [Jesus]" begins with salvation. A marriage cannot be "in the Lord" when one is outside that

---

4. For more on this see my exposition of Proverbs 31 in *Christian Living in the Home.*

salvation sphere. What is prohibited, therefore, is any marriage with an unbeliever.

Throughout Old Testament history there is a record of marriages to unbelieving partners consistently turning God's people away from Him. When Paul insists that we must not be "unequally yoked together with unbelievers," he refers not only to marriage, but to all close relationships. However, since marriage is the closest of all relationships, surely marriage is included in the prohibition. To be unequally yoked is to be unable to pull together. That means two divergent standards, two opposite goals, two radically differing interpretations of life, two incompatible masters to serve, and two contrary powers at work. Unbelief allied with belief in Christ means just one thing—there can be no real intimacy in matters that really count. The one-flesh ideal is defeated. The two cannot pull together because they are not truly together.[5]

Counselors must make these matters clear in pre-marital counseling where mixed marriages are contemplated. And they must keep them in mind where believers have already violated God's prohibition. In such cases, the directions of I Corinthians 7:12-16 are crucial. The believer will need to repent of sin and work toward all that God intends for him or her, as a witness before the unconverted partner (on this see also I Pet. 3:1-7).

Conclusion

A marriage counselor who cares to help others must not only have his own thinking straight, but also be aware of the false concepts that make havoc of marriages—even

5. On the importance of marrying "only in the Lord," see Dorothy Voshell's fine work, *Whom Shall I Marry?* (Phillipsburg, N.J.: Presbyterian and Reformed, 1979).

among Christians. A thorough acquaintance with the errors exposed in these chapters, their biblical alternatives, and ways of showing married couples their biblical responsibilities is necessary for counselors to spare couples of many problems sabotaging marriages today.

Assignment

From this and the previous chapter compile a list of *all* of the errors mentioned, in the form of a ready reference chart to which you may later refer during counseling itself. (Such lists are often conveniently placed under a glass top on one's desk.) Next to each error listed, mention the verse or two verses that you will probably use most frequently when discussing the problem.   Do a thorough job in making this list; you will find it helpful for years to come. The list may be scanned at a glance, while counseling, to remind you to explore various areas of conceptual error that otherwise you might have forgotten.

6
Sinful Living Patterns In General

Rather than repeat what I have said elsewhere, I refer you to the appropriate chapters in *The Christian Counselor's Manual* for a definitive study of the biblical way to help people discover sinful living patterns and exchange them for righteous ones. Here let me simply say, it is not a matter of breaking habits, but of replacing them with biblical alternatives. The Scriptures speak in Colossians 3, for instance, not only of "putting off" the old ways but of "putting on" the new ones. This put-off, put-on dynamic is basic to replacing sinful patterns. Colossians declares that "in Christ" we have already exchanged the old for the new, and that our daily living patterns should increasingly conform to that new status we already have in Him. We are to become (now) in actual living what we are (already) in Christ.

Why am I concerned here about sinful living patterns developed before or during marriage? Because they are a destructive force in the marriage. In no way can marriage counseling be successful until the counselor becomes aware of their harmful effects and learns how to combat them.

Before turning to a number of the more common and

significant patterns, in the following chapters, we must first discuss some general aspects of habitual sin within marriage.

Many counselors fail because they treat every problem like a one-time event. They do not recognize it as part of a habitual pattern. That is a serious failure. While it is true a husband may, for instance, commit adultery once, never having done so before, there likely was a habitually adulterous thought life leading up to the act. Unless the counselor is aware of this possibility and confronts it, his help in resolving the one-time incident may very well set the marriage up for future failure. Not that there is no such thing as a one-time sin, or that every sin is the latest manifestation of a habitual pattern. No, but often it is—more often than we may think.

That is why a counselor needs to inquire about similar instances in the past. You are not a Freudian who needs to uncover every flat stone in a person's history. But you do want to know if and how often the same sort of thing has happened before, whether in action or in thought. It is necessary to know whether you are dealing with a pattern or a one-time event.

What difference does it make? Why is it so important? Because patterns are more stubborn to dislodge. Since they are habitual, they are deceptive to both the counselee and the counselor. That is because habits are done unconsciously, smoothly, and automatically. And that is what makes habits so stubborn.

A habit is dislodged only by crowding it out with its biblical alternative. Counselors, therefore, must learn not only what the sinful habit patterns are, but what the biblical alternatives to each may be. They must be ready not only to suggest these, but also to carefully discipline counselees in the new patterns until they too become habitual.[1]

1. For more on helping counselees become disciplined, see *Ready to Restore* (Phillipsburg, N.J.: Presbyterian and Reformed, 1981).

Is Change Possible?

Some have taught that it is impossible to change people who have developed long-standing habits, especially those going back to childhood. The Bible teaches otherwise. It is central to our Christian faith that change is possible. No change commanded by God is unrealistic for those who know Christ as their Savior and are willing to do things His way. The results of an interesting study illustrate the biblical truth that even childhood patterns are not irrevocable. Harvard followed the lives of hundreds of men over a forty-year period. George Valliant, in a recently released book entitled *Adaptation to Life*, claims that the results of the study show that the quality of childhood had less to do with subsequent life than the patterns that were acquired later on, and that traumatic events in early life rarely mold individual lives. This is the central fact in Valliant's findings.[2]

Valliant's findings do not add credibility to the biblical teaching—it stands firm regardless of what men may say. Scripture needs no confirmation or support. But it is interesting that after the forty years, and all of the harm done by Freudian speculation about the impossibility, or near impossibility, of change after childhood, the study's findings should so clearly confute Freud's erroneous views.

Counselees will tell you, of course, that they cannot change. Their protestations are partly excuse making, partly the acceptance of Freudian ideas, and partly their own frustration after repeated failure to change. This failure usually stems from attempts to change by breaking habits (the world's one-factored method), rather than replacing them (God's two-factored means for producing change). It may also be the result of turning to additional unbiblical patterns, or seeking change by one's own strength rather than the power of the Holy Spirit.

2. Reported by Tim Hackler in *A.S.A. Magazine* (April, 1982), p. 104.

There are many other reasons why people claim change is impossible. Some say they are too old. To these, the counselor replies, "Let's consider what sorts of changes God was able to produce in Abraham when he was a lot older than you. . . ." There are those who plead childhood problems: "But you have no idea of the conditions in which I was raised. . . ." To them, the reply is, "Perhaps I don't, but do you think the conditions in Corinth or in Thessalonica were much better? God required change from Christians converted out of paganism and got it. He requires the same of you, and by His grace, you too will change." Still others plead genetic problems; many of these typify a renewed interest in "temperament." To them you must say, "Temperament studies do not come from the Bible. They go back to pagan Greek thought that postulated the four-humor theory of temperament. The Bible cares nothing for such teachings about temperament. If temperament were as important as some seem to think, the Bible would be filled with it. Instead, there isn't even a whisper of such concern in the Scriptures. You can change; temperament has nothing to do with it." Still others protest, "But that's just the way I am," meaning thereby, "Don't expect me to change." To them the reply is, "Doubtless that is the way you are, but that is not the way God wants you to be, and if you will only confess your sin and do as He says, that is not the way you will be in the future."

At all costs, counselors must be firm on the central fact that dramatic change is possible—in Christ. And they must just as firmly maintain the obligation to make every change that is demanded by the Bible. There is hope in every command; God commands nothing of His people that, using His Word, in the power of His Spirit, they cannot fulfill—if they only will. It is the task of every counselor to help those who wish to do God's will to do so, and it is his task to bring conviction to those who don't or who make excuses that cannot be upheld by the Bible.

Now that we have discussed this point, we may turn to specific patterns that will be met in marriage counseling.

Assignment

The wife says, "I'm a night person," while the husband protests, "Yes, and I'm a day person." They claim that is why they have very little communication, and no children. You tell them, "Well, then, one or the other of you must change, or you both must change a little." They both reply, "Oh, but we can't. That's just the way we are, you see; there is no way in which we can change. We have tried." Write a thorough discussion of this problem from a biblical point of view, describing what can be done to rectify it. You may wish to set up your paper in the form of a counseling session.

In addition, make a list of all the biblical put-offs and put-ons that you can discover. They may or may not be found in the *form* of "put off . . . ," "put on. . . ." Bring these to class and share them with other members of the group.

7
Particular Sinful Living Patterns:
Part One

In the previous chapter, we discussed a number of the common excuses people raise to justify their sinful living patterns. The thrust of those excuses is that the kind of change demanded by the Scriptures is not possible. A counselor must confront that objection if he is going to help his counselees. We have already dealt in general with how to do so. It is now necessary to consider several of the principal problems, and how to handle them.

Communication Breakdown

The communication breakdown that occurred when Adam sinned had both a vertical and a horizontal dimension. Before that, perfect communication had sustained the relationships between God and man, and between the man and his wife. The break in verbal fellowship between God and man was so great that it radically altered the fellowship between Adam and Eve. Communication is essential to all human relationships, but it is especially important for developing and maintaining the deep intimacy that God designed for the marriage relationship.

As I have pointed out in the previous chapter, self-disclosure is essential to friendship and, in particular, to intimacy. When Adam and Eve sinned, they covered their bodies because they suddenly felt vulnerable; they had something to hide. Unconfessed and unforgiven sin always leads to a cover-up with its inevitable consequence: a breakdown in one's relationship with others. So Adam and Eve ran and hid from God. People do the same thing today. But they also run from one another. Husbands hide from their wives, and wives cover up parts of their lives, when there is unresolved sin. In order to establish or reestablish communication in intimacy, it is first necessary to eliminate the sin that is blocking communication. Every counselor needs to remember that fact, as well as the very strong probability that a communication breakdown is part of a habitual pattern of noncommunication.

That is why Paul speaks of the communication problem in terms of the put-off, put-on dynamic:

> So then, putting off lying, each one must speak truth with his neighbor, since we are members of one another (Eph. 4:25).

Until lying patterns have been replaced by patterns of truth telling, there is no hope for solving the communication problem.

Notice that before Paul takes up the three authority relations discussed in Ephesians 5 and 6, he deals first with communication in 4:25-32. He does this because he is well aware that in order to walk together (as husband and wife, parents and children, or master and slave), Christians must first know how to talk together. The Christian's walk—the great subject of Ephesians 4–6—is not a solitary walk. And harmony in walk requires harmony in talk.

That presents a question about what I have called "the communication dilemma": If communication is necessary to solve problems, *including the communication problem*, how do we resolve this dilemma?

Matthew 18:15-20, among other texts, addresses itself to the difficulty. First, two parties alone—they may be a husband and wife—attempt to resolve a difficulty. But if one "will not listen," then the other is to go and get one or two other brothers to intercede as counselors. If he refuses to listen, then the matter is taken to the church. If he will not hear the church, he is excommunicated. The operative phrase in this pattern is "if he refuses to listen." A communication breakdown is at issue here. What is the answer to the dilemma at each step? To bring in others to facilitate communication, thus leading to reconciliation.

When two parties can no longer resolve their differences and communication breaks down, they need to call for help. Others can step in and hold together the wires that have been snipped by sin long enough to get communication going again.

Mishandled anger is one of the principal hindrances to communication, as Paul indicates in Ephesians 4:26. Anger manifests itself in two sinful ways: clamming up (v. 26) and blowing up (vv. 29-32). Both are wrong, even when the anger itself is not sinful. Because I have dealt with these matters in depth elsewhere, I shall not elaborate on them here.

Every counselor must be prepared to discuss anger, lying, the put-off, put-on dynamic, and such matters, if he wishes to help husbands and wives reestablish communication.[1] And, he must know how to use the principles that he learns in practical, effective ways.

---

1. For more on clamming up and blowing up, see *Competent to Counsel, The Christian Counselor's Manual*, and *Christian Living in the Home*.

In the Preface, I mentioned that well-meaning Christians sometimes give advice that is almost as bad as the problems themselves. One example is in the book, *Just Talk to Me*, where Andre Bustanoby offers what he calls "the cardinal rule of communication: *my position is not better than, but different from yours.*"[2] That is certainly not the cardinal rule in Ephesians 4! There, the cardinal rule is to speak the truth. If the tactic recommended by Bustanoby were followed consistently by counselees, it would probably lead to at least these two sorry results:

1. Lying.
2. Inculcating the humanistic idea that truth is relative, that one person's "truth" is as good as another's.

Both of these results are dangerous. If I say to my wife that my position is not better than hers, just different, I may be lying, because my position may actually be better (hers may be sinful); and, whether it is better or not, if I *think* it is and yet follow Bustanoby's lead, I am still lying because I am saying something contrary to what I believe is true.

Moreover, if I follow Bustanoby, I end up concluding that it doesn't matter what you believe, just as long as you are sincere. The important thing is peace, at any cost—even at the cost of truth. What's true for you may not be true for me, and visa versa. So there's no sense making an issue of it.

You can see what that view does to the absolute truth of Scripture. The Bible's cardinal rule of communication is "speak the truth in love." And often the truth hurts. But that is no reason for not speaking it. Two people united in the bonds of biblical intimacy can never settle for dodging the issues. They must come to grips with what God wants them to believe and do, whether that accords with the views of one party or neither. As Paul says, "We are members of one another." That means both parties must share the

2. (Grand Rapids: Zondervan, 1981), p. 38 (his emphasis).

truth. Unless they can be "agreed," how can they walk together? They can't. They need to be able to resolve differences from God's Word, not avoid them. The truth may hurt, but, in the long run, it will not hurt like a lie.

Speak truth, and not in uncontrolled anger—that is Paul's message in Ephesians 4. Any truth can be told to another, if it is relevant and spoken in the right manner. Paul refers to this as speaking "constructively" words that "help" rather than words that tear down (Eph. 4:29). This is part of what is meant by telling the truth in love.

I am not implying that a husband or wife may never say what Bustanoby recommends. But the occasions on which such a statement may be made are limited to the following:

1. When it is true.
2. When the difference in positions has to do with preference or expediency.

Never can one settle for what Bustanoby recommends when a matter of biblical principle is at stake. While there are times when, after adequate study and discussion of biblical principles, no immediate decision can be reached, and two parties must settle *for the moment* to agree to disagree, it is never with the idea that both contradictory positions are equally good, and only different.

Speaking the truth constructively, with words designed to help another, is the cardinal rule of communication and will, in the long run, bring about proper relationships between a husband and wife. Do not get wrapped up in psychological gimmicks; teach people what God's Word requires of them and help them begin to follow it, no matter how unattractive that may at first seem.

Self-Centeredness

Perhaps the central pattern in all marital problems is

self-centeredness.[3] Paul mentions this sinful pattern of life in II Timothy 3:2:

People will be self-centered, money-seekers. . . .

The word *philautos* in this passage literally means "a lover, or friend of one's self." It is bad enough that we are selfish in our sinful human nature, but today psychologists and psychiatrists systematically encourage and justify self-centeredness. The emphasis on being "number one" or "looking out for number one" runs all through our society. You can hear it at the football games (even at the local Christian school), you can read dozens of books written by Christians who tell you that you are really "somebody," and you can find full-blown programs for enhancing your self-image by becoming assertive. Society today has institutionalized selfishness!

Of course you will be told that selfishness and self-love are two different things. But you cannot find the distinction in the Scriptures. People who like to push the self-image, self-love concept often will tell you that Jesus commanded us to love ourselves. They will turn to the two great commandments and triumphantly point out that Jesus ordered us to love our neighbors *as we love ourselves*. But they distort the Scriptures in doing so. Here is why:

1. There is no command to love one's self; the presupposition underlying the command to love our neighbors as ourselves is that we already love ourselves. The last phrase might even be translated "as [you are loving] yourself."

2. Jesus Himself says, "On these two command-

3. Keep in mind that any or all of the above patterns, as well as those yet to be considered, may interweave. Frequently, self-centeredness and lack of discipline are found in combination with other patterns. Never stop gathering data until you are sure that a pattern is not accompanied by self-centeredness and/or lack of discipline. For chapters of material on data gathering, see *The Christian Counselor's Manual*.

ments . . . ," thereby making it beyond dispute that He summed up the law in only *two* commandments (love God; love neighbor), not three. Yet, in spite of Christ's unmistakable pronouncement that there were two commandments, many go on declaring not only that there are three, but that unless we learn how to love ourselves we will never be able to love another.

The marriage counselor will discover that the combination of native self-centeredness and the added impetus given by current psychological propaganda is a fundamental problem in marriages everywhere. He must be prepared to counter any seemingly plausible justification of self-centeredness, especially twisted and biased interpretations of the Scriptures. In addition, he must be able to set forth the true biblical position on the matter.

Jesus told us plainly that "whoever wants to save his life will lose it, but whoever loses his life for My sake will find it" (Matt. 16:25). As He declared in the preceding verse, we must "deny" self, putting it to death on the cross. That is the key to having a good self-image. But, notice, the good self-image comes only by becoming a good self. The more one obeys the two commandments to love God and neighbor, the better his self-image will become.

Self-esteem is a by-product; it may not be pursued for its own sake, either directly or indirectly. If a person tries to obey Christ's two commandments *in order to obtain a good self-image*, he will fail. One may not obey God as a gimmick. He accepts no such obedience; we must obey "from the heart" (Rom. 6:17). Obedience as a gimmick leads to hypocrisy, which creates a totally unbiblical self-image.

Those who throw themselves into the service of Christ, putting Him and His kingdom before all else, find that, in the long run, God honors them, adding benefits that others vainly seek as ends in themselves. It is a question of whether to serve self or Christ, creature or Creator, the by-product itself or the Giver of every perfect gift. Counselors must call a halt to pursuits of good self-image, self-esteem, and self-love (institutionalized manifestations of self-centeredness) and send their counselees back to good, old-fashioned, heart-felt, obedient service to Christ in His kingdom.

That self-centeredness is destructive to marriage goes without saying. When two parties come together who want what they want and expect others to give it to them, you have all of the ingredients for trouble. The essence of married love, to which each party pledges himself or herself, is to put the other first. That is the opposite of self-centeredness. Those who have developed self-centered life-styles will not find that easy to do. Certainly, it will not happen automatically and in most cases will take concerted, prayerful effort to bring about. Most often, this effort will have to begin with a recognition of one's sinful ways and repentance. That spirit of repentance, which seeks to put away old ways and put on new ones, is what is necessary for making the change.

When Jesus tells us to take up the cross "daily," and thus put to death our own desires, and to "follow" Him instead (Luke 9:23), He sets forth the basic put-on, put-off dynamic that is essential to making the change. That change consists of putting God's will above our own. To do that, we must also put others and their concerns above ours, because that is a part of God's will. Love for God and one's neighbor (the closest neighbor being one's spouse) means that love for self will have to be put aside.

Because the vows and subsequent challenges of marriage so clearly demand a renunciation of self in order to put another human being first, marriage counters self-centeredness more than any other human institution. No wonder sinners have so much difficulty in marriage: Its very design—that of living for someone else to make him or her happy and meet his or her need for companionship—is contrary to sinful human nature. No human being, not even a redeemed one, can keep the vows of marriage without divine guidance and power. God has wonderfully given Christians both. His Word guides us and His Spirit enables us to walk according to its directions. It is the counselor's task to help counselees recognize and avail themselves of these provisions for a marriage that reflects Christ's relationship to His church.

Since this chapter has grown long, we will continue our look at the principal living patterns that cause difficulties in marriage, in the next chapter.

Assignment

Do an exegetical study of all of the passages having to do with self, love of self, denial of self, and self-crucifixion. Relate your results to the problems of marriage in a paper to hand in.

Describe a typical communication breakdown as it occurs in a marriage counseling session, and show how a skillful biblical counselor might handle it.

8
Particular Sinful Living Patterns: Part Two

In the previous chapter I considered two sinful living patterns responsible for much marriage failure: communication breakdown and self-centeredness. In this chapter, I shall continue to look at common patterns with which marriage counselors must familiarize themselves, particularly lack of discipline, money problems, blame shifting, and wrong priorities.

But, before turning to each of these, let me emphasize that just as sins are often manifestations of patterns, so also sinful patterns often come in combinations of pairs, triplets, or more. A person lacking discipline, for instance, will almost always have money problems because of his failure to control his spending or keep good records, or both. A person with wrong priorities will often, as a result, have money problems. Someone who shifts blame to his or her spouse will foster communication problems in the process. And, as I have already shown, communication problems can lead to the deepening of all other problems.

Such patterns become more and more entangled with each other as they are allowed to grow. One unchecked problem leads to another, and so on. But, conversely, as biblical counseling confronts and solves one problem, that leads to the solution of others. Overcoming one problem gives the counselee strength for meeting the next. Moreover, the basic biblical dynamic for meeting and solving problems soon becomes a learned pattern itself, which may be generalized for solving any other problem that may arise.

So remember to inquire about all the patterns mentioned in these two chapters (they are the most common ones), as well as any others that may be present.

Lack of Discipline

Because I have devoted some space to this matter in *Ready to Restore,* I shall not duplicate what I said there. Here, I am concerned about the effects of undisciplined living on marriage. In *Ready to Restore* my concern was to show that a counselee must be taught discipline in order to replace an old pattern with a new one. There I also stressed the need for counselors to be (or become) disciplined themselves in order to teach others discipline. Discipline problems, like communication problems, give rise to a dilemma: It takes discipline to practice and eventually establish any new pattern—including the pattern of discipline. So, to help undisciplined persons become disciplined, the counselor must at first "ride herd" on their progress, setting up a heavy structure for them and monitoring their progress closely.

I have said that lack of discipline can lead to money troubles. But because discipline is essential to all that we do, its lack can cause difficulty in any other area of the marriage as well. Take, for instance, so simple a matter as doing the laundry. Great rifts in marriages can come from bitter words spoken over a wife's failure to have her husband's shirts ready when he needs them for work. Not paying bills on time can lead to marriage disasters. In general, putting off responsibilities is one of the principal causes of problems. Counselors must therefore know how to discuss the biblical principles of scheduling and living according to plan. In doing so, they will point out the fact that the God in whose image we are created is a God who plans and schedules. Christ's coming was according to a schedule laid out in Daniel; His work was in accord with prophecies, types, and shadows that prefigured His advent, in some cases, by millennia. If God schedules, who is man to think he need not?

Counselors will be wise to ask about patterns of undisciplined living and to observe carefully how well homework is done. Failure to complete homework on time is one indication of lack of discipline. Such failure calls for more than a reprimand or a bare exhortation. The counselee needs help in disciplining his week to assure completion of homework. Counselors should not be too prone to charge their counselees with rebellion or a lack of concern. Some counselees are so undisciplined that, even with the best of intentions, they nevertheless fail because they do not know how to approach their assignments in a disciplined fashion.

I have spoken often, elsewhere, about the importance of *how to*. A person needs to know not only what to do, but also how to do it. The same injunction applies to discipline —with added emphasis. Not only must an undisciplined person be taught the principles of disciplined living and how to apply them, but, in addition, he must be monitored to be sure that he continues to do what he should, according to plan.

A counselee might not even realize his lack of discipline causes other problems. We must not excuse him for his lack of discipline. But we should understand the part it plays in his failure. Moreover, we must recognize it as both a prime problem in its own right, and a very common complicating problem as well. Look for it, not to provide an excuse, but to help the counselee fully overcome its insidious consequences.

Money Problems

It needs to be emphasized that money itself does not cause problems. To say, as some commonly have, that "money is the root of all evil" is a serious misquotation and misrepresentation of Scripture. What does the Bible really teach? Listen to Paul as he writes in I Timothy 6:10:

For love of money is a root of all sorts of evils.

The verse teaches neither that money *itself* is the root of evil nor that it is the root of *all* evil. What it says is that the *love* of money is *a* root of any and every sort of evil. You could not, given the time and data, trace back every evil that ever occurred to money, or even to the love of it. Surely, evil results from other factors as well. The point is that every sort of evil has been committed by man because of his love of money. Men have killed, lied, committed adultery, made idols, broken the sabbath, and more—all for money. You can go down the entire list of the Ten Commandments and show that every one of them has been broken for the love of money.

In a marriage where there is a money tangle, you want to find out, first, whether the *love* of money is its cause. Then, if you discover greed, a miserly attitude, or a mad drive to get money, the biblical lead suggests that there may well be other "sorts of evils" to be dealt with.

As Paul observes, those who are eager for money have even "wandered from the faith and have pierced themselves through with many sorrows" (I Tim. 6:10b). Such sorrow is not uncommon among counselees. And yet counselors have all too rarely made use of this powerful passage to bring counselees to conviction and repentance.

At an appropriate point, a counselor may need to ask his counselee, "As a life goal, have you 'determined to be rich'?" If the answer is yes, the counselor may also read to him the verse preceding the one I have just quoted:

> . . . but those who determine to be rich fall into temptation and a trap and into many injurious desires that plunge people into ruin and destruction (I Tim. 6:9).

That is both a powerful warning and a prudent insight. The decision to become rich leads to the pursuit of money, in which many temptations to "all sorts of evils" present themselves as short cuts to achieving the goal. Notice it does not say that if a person determines to be rich, he *may* fall into temptation, or foolish and injurious desires *may* trap him; no, it says that these things *will* happen! That means that it is not a Christian ideal to set one's heart on becoming rich. Indeed, because this is a biblically unworthy pursuit, we are warned that it will only lead to more and more serious consequences—possibly even wandering away from the faith.[1]

Counselors must note that it is not only the wealthy who tend to make money their goal and their love. A desire for money is often just as intense in those who have little or none of it. So, it isn't how much money one has or doesn't have that is important, but his attitude toward money. The critical questions are: Does he love money? Has he made the acquisition of money a goal of life? This is the counselor's concern.

Frequently, as the passage implies, the counselor will discover that behind sinful patterns such as lying and hatred

---

1. See also Prov. 28:20, 22; 23:4. According to Jesus, the Pharisees were "money lovers" (Luke 16:14).

is the love of money. The counselor should therefore look for ways in which the money problem may be tied in with any other sin. Such a tie does not always exist; but more often than might be supposed, the love of money and the determination to have it lies behind the particular sin. That oft-neglected connection requires careful questioning in order for the counselor to bring it to the surface.

In hard economic times, such as those in which I am writing, the temptations for Christians to become involved in shady money-making deals is great. And today there are many organizations, some of which claim biblical support for their views, that tell people that the pursuit of money as a life goal is a worthy cause. Such teaching is untrue and very dangerous, as the passage before us makes clear. While having money and even enjoying money (cf. 6:17b), if God sends it, is not wrong at all, the love of money and the determination as a goal of life that "I shall be rich" is a sin that can lead to many others.

While we are on the subject, it is important to enlarge just a bit on the point that having riches is not wrong. Paul discusses the matter of riches in I Timothy 6:17-19:

> Authoritatively instruct the rich of this present age not to be haughty, nor to set their hope on the uncertainty of riches, but rather on God, Who richly provides everything for our enjoyment. They must do good, be rich in good deeds, be ready to give, generous, laying up the treasure of a good foundation for the future so that they may lay hold on the life that is really life.

That is the vital passage on riches. Note that it does not teach rich persons to give away all of their possessions, or even such a significant part of them that they will no longer be rich. Throughout the discussion, Paul assumes that they will continue to be rich. Nor does it teach that the enjoyment of what riches can bring is wrong; indeed, it affirms the opposite. But what it does say plainly, in addition to what we have already seen regarding life goals, is that one must not become a snob because of his money; that he must not depend on his money, but on God; that he must be generous in sharing what he has with those who are truly in need; and that he must focus his attention on the kind of true riches you can send ahead of you for the world to come.

Some counselees violate every one of these biblical principles. But if even one of these money principles is violated in a marriage, it will bring "sorrow" to the home. Usually in a home where there are money problems, you will find squabbles between the husband and the wife over how money should be spent. Such a problem often has deeper roots. You will likely discover a life commitment to making money, a dependence on money rather than on God (often manifested by inordinate fear having to do with money), a failure to give to others (disclosed by the fact that one's money doesn't satisfy because he has missed the blessings of giving), or haughty attitudes. Until this basic issue is dealt with, the surface problem will resist permanent solution.

Most Christians need to be "authoritatively instructed" about money. Since they have not been taught properly, they do not know how to put biblical principles into practice. As a marriage counselor, not only must you have these principles firmly fixed in your own mind, but you must be able to share them in the full exercise of biblical authority with those you counsel. If such instruction were not necessary, then Paul would not have ordered Timothy to give it.

The counselor must be especially careful not to allow a rich counselee's wealth to interfere with the necessary task of confronting him with biblical principles. Timothy was to do just that—instruct the rich of this world. A careful reading of all that James has to say about riches and rich persons, as well as how the church ought to treat the rich, is indispensable for every biblical counselor. If we are not careful, we will show an unjustified deference to rich persons, which is detrimental both to them and to the church of Jesus Christ.

Now and then husbands and wives will differ strongly over whether it is right to have and enjoy an abundance of money. That controversy stems from a current emphasis on "the simple life" that is entirely unbiblical. Those who view simple living to be an obligation for all must be taught the proper attitude toward and use of riches; like Paul, they may need to "know how to abound" (Phil. 4:12). As he says in I Timothy 6:17, it is God "Who richly provides everything for our enjoyment."

Part of the enjoyment of having riches is in sharing them, using them to do good to others. Until a counselee has learned that "it is more blessed to give than to receive," his marriage will be plagued with the sorrows that wrong attitudes toward riches will bring. But equally important, he must learn how to enjoy God's good gifts and not withhold thanksgiving to God because someone has sold him a bill of sociological goods under the name of Christianity.

The ways money can cause problems in a marriage are too numerous to explore here. Of greatest importance is getting a firm hold on the clearest principles and learning to implement them in any given case.[2] Every counselor ought to have a method for helping counselees budget their funds, or he should know some person to whom he may refer counselees for financial advice. (A Christian businessman whose approach to finances is fully scriptural would be a great asset to any pastor's counseling.)

Blame Shifting

When God questioned Adam and Eve after the fall, their

2. For complete directions on how to implement general principles in particular cases, see my book, *Insight and Creativity in Christian Counseling* (Phillipsburg, N.J.: Presbyterian and Reformed, 1982).

response was the first instance of blame shifting in history. What happened then has been going on ever since. "The woman that You gave me, she . . ." was Adam's complaint. For Eve it was "the serpent, he. . . ." Husbands and wives who come for marriage counseling almost always have similar things to say.

Adam and Eve chose to shift their blame onto God, one another, and external circumstances in their environment, which God had created. In the final analysis, however, all of their blame shifting amounted to this: It is God's fault.

A counselor can expect to hear such things as, "If only my wife/husband were to do (or not do) so-and-so, then I would do (or not do) thus-and-so." That is the essence of blame shifting. It is deflecting one's guilt, whether from sins of commission or sins of omission, onto another.

The wise counselor will, at the very first inklings of blame shifting, sort out the fundamental responsibilities of each party. He will say something like this: "Now wait a minute. Certainly it would be easier to do so-and-so if your spouse did thus-and-so, but you must do so-and-so whether he/she does thus-and-so or not. You don't do it in order to get your spouse to do what you'd like to see him/her do, or only on the condition that he/she does it; you do it because God expects you to, and because you have promised unconditionally to do so in your marriage vows." That point must be clear. Each party in the marriage has responsibilities that are his or hers before God and the other. He or she must be held responsible for assuming those responsibilities, *regardless of what anyone else does or fails to do*. That is what sorting out the responsibilities means.

Any counselor who allows blame shifting will fail. But the counselor who states explicitly at the outset that God will not let us shift our responsibilities to another will be on the right track from the start.

Wrong Priorities

Ephesians and Colossians indicate that the order of a married person's priorities is spouse, then children, then job. Sinners tend to change these priorities. A man is likely to put his job before his wife, children, or both. A wife is likely to put the children in a higher place than her husband.

God is not on the list of priorities. He is not one piece of the pie; He is over the whole pie. We must put God first in all things by obeying what His Word says in every area.

Much more will be said regarding priorities when we consider marriage roles. Here you may find the following chart helpful for enabling counselees to analyze their present priorities and develop more biblical ones for the future. Hand out a sheet of paper like the sample shown here, and ask the counselee to list what his priorities are and ought to be.

Priorities

Current Priorities	Unprofitable items to remove	Items to add	Items from Col. 1,3 in order of biblical priority

Since sinful living patterns can cause great difficulty in a marriage, a counselor must be well aware of the major problem areas and ready to deal with each in depth.

Assignment

Consider the discipline in your own life. Is it adequate? If not, draw up a plan for becoming the disciplined person that God wants you to be in order to help others.

Locate and revise a budget program that would help others analyze and allocate their finances as good stewards of God's good gifts.

List 25 failures for which a husband or wife is likely to shift the blame to his or her spouse.

9

The Importance of Relationships with Others

We have looked, so far, at erroneous concepts and sinful living patterns as proximate causes of marriage problems. We now turn to an often neglected area—the influence of outside relationships on a marriage.

The negative influence of others on a marriage can sometimes be so strong that it destroys the marriage. It is not blame shifting to say that influences can be that powerful. An influence is literally "a flowing into." It consists of a flowing in of ideas and pressures. All our contacts with others inevitably influence us one way or the other. That is because God made us interdependent creatures.

The reason we may not shift blame onto others is that we are responsible for the influences to which we subject ourselves. We need not allow any harmful influence to capture and direct our minds. The Bible not only warns us to avoid evil influences, but tells us how to do so. Influences are a matter of choice, even when we are not conscious of their effects on us, since the Bible has set forth adequate warning of what we should avoid. So, while influences are inevitable and powerful, we may not shift blame if we expose ourselves to the wrong *kind* of influences. God holds us responsible to avoid evil influences and to seek out edifying ones.

That is why it is so important to choose a Christian wife or husband, who really cares about living for Christ. And that is why it is essential for a married couple to belong to a solid, Bible-believing church, to study the Scriptures, and to choose friends who will exert a positive influence on their marriage.

I say that we are creatures of influence because everywhere in the Bible it is assumed that we will be influenced for good or ill. For instance, in III John 11 we are commanded:

Dear friend, don't imitate evil, but imitate good.

We are not told, "If you happen to decide to imitate, then choose good models, not evil ones." No, nothing of the sort. It is presupposed that we will imitate somebody. So, we are told that we are responsible to choose carefully *whom* we imitate.

Why is imitation inevitable? Because imitation is a large part of the human learning process. Most of the things that a child learns before going to school are by imitation. That is why we speak English and not Chinese. That is also why one American speaks with a southern accent and another with a general American or eastern accent. Imitation is a necessary characteristic of human nature. God created us in such a way that much of what we learn comes through imitation, both in childhood and throughout life. And that is good. But as sinners, we use a good process for evil ends.

Marriage counselors have not adequately stressed the effects of evil influences on a marriage. It is time to make the point clearly that whenever a couple or one spouse develops a close tie with someone whose influence is evil, that will inevitably affect the marriage for ill. Because of the intimacy of the "one-flesh" relationship, what happens to one happens also to the other. Counselors, therefore, need to be aware of the problem and to gather adequate information about friends and associates.

The influence of another man at work, filling a husband's ears with stories of sexual exploits, can lead to ruin. The impact of a neighbor who hangs on the phone three afternoons a week and encourages talk about how terrible husbands are may unsettle a marriage. The influence of in-laws or the words and ideas of children, if allowed to turn one spouse against the other, can be most destructive. But such influences *can* be avoided. One need not listen. Biblical warnings about purity of mind and mouth, about gossip, and about putting down others behind their backs would themselves eliminate the influences if properly heeded.

Other scriptural commands apply even more explicitly to the influence of ungodly persons. Take, for instance, the statement in I Corinthians 15:33:

> Don't be misled; "Bad companions corrupt good habits."

There Paul makes it clear that it is easy to be misled in regard to companions. A person may think he is strong enough to withstand the influences of another, while gradually his own standards erode almost imperceptibly. He is "misled." Another may reason, "I'll spend time with an evildoer to help him," but ends up more influenced than influencing. He too is misled. Since it is easy to be misled, an association ought not to be maintained unless one plainly influences another for good. And, even in those cases where the influence for good is dominant, the value of the association will be proportional to the rate and extent that the befriended person is directed to Christ.

Just as any close companionship influences one either for good or for evil, so too one party either is influencing another or is being influenced by him. The situation is neither neutral nor static. The boat never sits still in the river; either it is going upstream against the current or it is drifting with it. Marriage counselors hear arguments to the contrary all the time. But they must be ready to reply with the warning, "Don't be misled."

Note also, Paul does not merely say that companions are influential: they are capable of corrupting the good already established in one's life. That is of great importance to the Christian counselor. Even if he has been succeeding in his counseling, the evil words of a close companion can turn everything around overnight.

Scriptural Warnings

There are many explicit biblical warnings about the influence of the teaching and example of others. Let me note just three New Testament warnings before looking at several found in the Book of Proverbs.

First, Romans 16:17, 18:

> Now I urge you, brothers, to watch out for those who, by disregarding the teaching that you have learned, cause divisions and give occasion for stumbling. Such people don't serve our Lord Christ as His slaves, but are slaves of their own appetites; and by fine talk and flattery they deceive the hearts of the unsuspecting.

In those two verses, there is a wealth of warning. First we are told that the wrong kind of associates can cause divisions. The warning applies no less to marriages than to churches. Often husbands and wives are divided by outside associations that give occasion for stumbling. Such influences present the temptation to sin. Drinking companions, gossips, homosexual solicitors—the variety is endless—all take their toll. And notice how they do it: by fine talk and flattery. They don't express their aims up front. Instead, by smooth words, subtleties, and flattery, they deceive the hearts of those who don't realize what is going on ("the unsuspecting"). It is clear how one ought to respond: "Watch out for" them. Don't be taken in by their flattery. Keep yourself from any close associations with them. If they don't serve Christ, they will not serve your marriage either.

In I Corinthians 5:9-11, we read,

> I wrote to you in my letter not to get mixed up with those who are sexually immoral; not that you shouldn't have anything whatever to do with the sexually immoral of this world (or with greedy persons, or robbers, or idolaters) since to do that you would have to leave the world altogether. But now let me explain that what I wrote was that you must not get mixed up with any so-called brother who is sexually immoral, or greedy, or an idolater, or a slanderer, or a drunkard or a robber; you must not even eat with a person like that.

Here, at the stage of discipline where the church must deal with a member ("tell it to the church"), there should be no close contact with the unrepentant sinner, *even though he is still considered a brother*. The world must be avoided, Paul says, but not in any stand-off fashion that prohibits regular business contacts and witnessing. Similarly, Christians should have no fellowship with other Christians while they are unrepentant. That doesn't mean they cannot be exhorted; Matthew 18 makes it clear that that is exactly what they need. But there is no true fellowship with someone who remains unrepentant. The faithful brothers, therefore, must not "get mixed up with" such a person.

The very same idea is expressed in II Thessalonians 3:14, 15:

> Now, whoever doesn't obey what we say in this letter, mark that person and don't mix with him so that he may become ashamed of himself. And yet, don't regard him as an enemy, but rather counsel him as a brother.

Clearly again, a believer is to look out for and mark such a
person—he is not to "mix" with him. Close association and
fellowship cannot be continued so long as the brother continues in his sin.

We need look at only a few of the Proverbs to get the idea
that it is dangerous to associate closely with people who
may be an evil influence:

> Quit the company of the simple and live (Prov. 9:6).
>
> The companion of fools will suffer harm (Prov. 13:20).
>
> Do not associate with one given to anger, and with a
> wrathful man do not keep company, lest you learn his
> ways and fall into a trap (Prov. 22:24).
>
> Be not among the winebibbers, among gluttonous eat-
> ers of flesh (Prov. 23:20).
>
> The partner of a thief hates himself; he heard the curse,
> but says nothing (Prov. 29:24).

Plainly, the same message comes across again and again:
Keep away from all whose lives are displeasing to God;
otherwise, you are likely to be influenced by them. That is
the consistent message of the Bible throughout the Old and
the New Testaments alike. It must be the consistent thrust
of the counselor as well. Bad influences not only weaken
and destroy marriages, but impede helpful counsel by pulling in the opposite direction. The problems a marriage
counselor must deal with are themselves enough of a challenge without an added tug of war with outside, opposing
forces.

Consequently, one of the first things a counselor should
determine is whether there is, in fact, any such outside
influence. If so, he should immediately seek a commitment
from his counselees to withdraw from any and all question-
able relationships. And following the double dynamic mentioned in a previous chapter, he should just as quickly help

them establish new relationships whose influence will edify them and strengthen their marriage.

We should now consider some particular persons who are likely to influence a marriage. That is the focus of the next chapter.

Assignment

Consider your own life. Think of all the persons who have had an influence on you, either for good or for evil. Make a list of them and what influence they had. This list may be useful when counseling others. Referring to it occasionally may provide some choice examples to illustrate a point in counseling.

Study the Scriptures further on the issue of influences, and write a paper discussing other passages that teach about the baneful effects of evil companions. Illustrate your discussion with examples you have known of in which marriages have been disrupted by the influence of others.

10
Particular Problem Relationships: Part One

In the preceding chapter I emphasized the powerful impact of personal associations on a marriage, and the biblical necessity to cut off all evil and injurious associations. Now my concern is to look more closely at some particular relationships that may be especially harmful to a married couple, and what, specifically, can be done about them.

In-Law Problems

Perhaps the most difficult of all relationships to deal with is the in-law relationship. It is true that you marry the family. Unlike other situations, you cannot simply avoid your in-laws if they are unsaved and their influence is unsavory; you must sustain the very best relationship possible toward them (Rom. 12:18). But, at the same time, you must not allow their influence to undermine your marriage in any way.

Probably the most important prerequisite for a proper

relationship with in-laws is a careful, intelligent, and prayer-ful application of the command found in Genesis 2:24:

> For this reason a man shall leave his father and his mother and adhere to his wife and they shall become one flesh.

The action commanded is to *leave;* the reason given is that a man and woman might become one flesh. Leaving and cleaving are both essential. Old ties cannot be broken unless there is "leaving." New ties cannot be established unless the old ones are gone. The loyalties, concerns, and author-ity structures that existed prior to the marriage must not be carried over unchanged into the marriage. A whole new relationship with one's parents must be established; nothing can be exactly the same as before. Marriage is a commitment to become a new person with brand new rela-tionships and responsibilities.

Often the break does not occur, is only partial, or is ragged, not a clean break. That is why a counselor needs to ascertain what a couple's relationship is to their parents and to their in-laws. If there has not been a complete break in the lines of authority, he may have to guide them through that step. Or if they have made the break in a non-Christian way, he may have to help them confess their sin and seek reconciliation. In any case, the proper relationship of a married couple to their parents is essential to a healthy marriage and ought therefore to be thoroughly explored in all marriage counseling.

Something else should be made clear: in-law troubles plague not only the recently married; sometimes they per-sist for thirty years!

One problem occurs when a husband depends on his father to make decisions for him rather than accept his responsibility as the head of a new and separate decision-making unit. While it is implied that a woman should "leave" her parents, the explicit call to "leave" father and mother is directed to the man. Why? Because he is to become the head of the new home, the one who is directly accountable to God for the decisions that govern that new authority structure.

It is especially bad when a man fails to sever the old ties enough to assume his new responsibilities. Not that he may not ask for or receive advice from his father. He should solicit advice when he thinks it may be helpful (not as a gimmick to "salve the old man"). But he must make his own decisions, whether they accord with the father's advice or not. Ultimately, he must stand or fall before the Lord.

It is of equal importance for the man to leave his mother. Here is where greater emotional ties often create problems. The proverbial apron strings are in all too many instances a reality, especially when the mother has not had an intimate relationship with her own husband. Often, such a woman looks to her sons for the satisfaction she ought to find in her husband. Therefore, she becomes very reluctant to let them go. Even after a son has left home, she tries to hold onto him. If he allows this, it will hurt not only his but his parents' marriage as well. He must make a clean, Christian break. Very frequently, counselors will find it necessary to guide him in doing so.

In some cases, children feel obligated to parents because of some financial loan or other transaction. The counselor will have to help the younger couple either repay the loan as quickly as possible (perhaps by taking out a loan elsewhere) or come to an understanding with the parents that while they are grateful for their help, this loan should not be allowed to interfere with the distinct authority structure of the new home. Parents must never try to "buy" the right to call the shots in their children's marriage. Marriage counselors often will need to bring in the in-laws with the children so that all receive biblical instruction. The situation is often too emotional for the children themselves to set it straight, especially if the in-laws simply won't listen to them.

In most instances, the husband is the key; if he does what God requires of him in Genesis, sooner or later, problems with his in-laws will be ironed out. Without the necessary perseverance to establish a proper relationship with one's in-laws, a damaging influence may be exerted on the marriage. Although in-laws rarely intend to cause harm, their sometimes thoughtless and self-seeking actions can produce more problems in the long run than an outright attack. Marriage counselors will find that, as usual, the quick, aboveboard approach, so feared by most people, will achieve the best and fastest results. While that may call for confrontations, and perhaps some emotional scenes, isn't it better to weather these now than to bear the unsettled and unsettling matter for months or even years? At some point the boil will burst anyway; better to prick it under controlled conditions and work for quick healing now.

I have mentioned that the young couple themselves may have some repenting to do. Often rough things are said shortly before or after the wedding that might never have been said except for the pressures of the occasion. Nevertheless, while this explains why rifts often coincide with marriage ceremonies, it does not excuse the wrong things said. If the couple has not dealt with such problems, it will be the counselor's duty to help them do so. They must seek forgiveness for any sinful thing they did or said at the time. Parents may harbor resentment over such remarks and acts for a long time. Forgiveness and reconciliation must not be delayed. Of course, parents may have some repenting to do also. If they are not Christians, however, that cannot be expected. Either way, the Christian couple must clear themselves before God and their in-laws. They must not repent and seek forgiveness as a ploy to obtain a similar response from their parents; they must do so because God expects them to, whatever the response may be.

Many other in-law problems can create stress and pressure for a marriage, but the basic factor in dealing with them all is to set up and maintain the biblical relationship found in Genesis 2. That will provide the proper background for meeting them all. Without it, every other in-law conflict will be a threat to the marriage. It is important to keep in mind that marriage is the greater and more basic relationship in the home. The child-parent relationship is temporary: God says it must be broken. The husband-wife relationship is permanent: God says it is to be lifelong and must not be broken. Keep these principles clear in your own thinking, help couples and their in-laws to see them clearly, and you will have gone a long way toward solving some of the principal dilemmas that might otherwise occur in the in-law relationship.

Children

The study of the home is not our interest in this book; but children do become a source of conflict between parents, and for that reason their influence on their parents deserves attention.

Many arguments have to do with children. Decisions must be made about them, and as little sinners, constantly present, they cause more than their share of problems. They are an influence from outside the marriage that is in the home itself.

Child discipline is perhaps the principal point of contention between parents. Here it is important to remember that the wife's task is to be a "helper." There are no limitations on that word in Genesis 2:18. It does not say that she is to be a helper in domestic chores only. Nothing of the sort. She is to help her husband in any and every way she can.

taking your wife's advice

That means giving him helpful advice when he requests it or seems to need it. It does not mean, however, that she may nag him with her opinions, or "advise" in nasty or demanding ways. The manner in which she advises must be truly helpful. The husband is to take this advice and consider it thoroughly in making decisions about discipline. If he cannot show biblically that her ideas are wrong and that his are right, he ought to give great heed to what she says. But he must make the final decision, and she must not contradict it—especially in front of the children. She must not undermine his discipline.

Sometimes the counselor will find that husbands do not discipline adequately. They expect their wives to do it all. They must be confronted with their fatherly duties, as described, for instance, in Ephesians 6. Marriage counselors must often help a couple to express their ideas on these matters (communication frequently breaks down over matters of child care) and develop an agreed-upon pattern of discipline in the home. Very frequently when that is done, all sorts of other good things happen. Because parents love their children and are concerned for their welfare, child care is a sensitive issue with the potential for destroying a marriage. Counselors must, therefore, investigate that area in any case of marital conflict.

Sometimes things have gone so far that the home is divided, husband against wife, and children lined up with one spouse or the other. The way they sit in the counseling room often indicates where the lines have been drawn. And the ensuing conversation confirms any suspicions about the domestic warfare and who is on which side.

It is a great tragedy: one parent dividing children against the other and against their brothers or sisters! Such parents must be taken aside, shown what they have done, and brought to repentance. Then, practical steps must be taken to bring about reconciliation in the home. Forgiveness must be asked of the children, as well as between them. Parents and children alike must agree to solve problems in a new and biblical way.[1]

Even after parents have been reconciled and are working together in the discipline of the home, one or more of the children may attempt to break up their newly found oneness. Here is why: <u>Over the years, the child has developed a pattern of getting what he wants by pitting one parent against the other. Now he sees that scheme coming to an end. He may therefore rebel against the new united front.</u> Counselors must anticipate this possibility and try to forestall it. But if it occurs anyway, they must advise the parents how to handle it. Obviously, the one essential thing is for the parents to refuse to allow the child to come between them again. They must remain united. That is the basic ground upon which they must stand if they are going to meet any challenge from their children. And that calls for the counselor to help them maintain their new unity, lest they fall back into the old pattern.

Much more may be said about conflicts over children, but this is enough to alert the wise counselor and direct him in the right path.[2] Since this chapter has grown long enough, the next will continue to discuss how particular relationships husbands and wives sustain with others can affect their marriages.

Assignment

Write a paper describing either an in-law or a child-care problem that is not mentioned in this chapter and that may negatively influence a marriage. Explain what a biblical counselor should do about it.

1. The "conference table," described in *Competent to Counsel*, may prove valuable for this purpose.

2. For flexibility and creativity in dealing with child-care problems, as well as any other, see my book, *Insight and Creativity in Christian Counseling*.

11

Particular Problem Relationships: Part Two

You might think there could not be a more emotional counseling circumstance than those considered in the previous chapter. But there is. Even more difficult than problems with in-laws and children are the inter-family tensions resulting from divorce.

A Former Spouse and Children

Divorce often carries with it all of the factors that made the former two relationships difficult and emotional, plus more. The impact is especially severe on the person who has lost both spouse and children. Sin causes misery, even to the nonoffending party in the divorce. He too must live with the consequences of his former spouse's disobedience to God.

One of the problems about divorce when children are involved is that it is not really the end. The aftereffects can be even more troublesome than the divorce itself. As one sees his or her children in an entirely different environ-

ment, torn between their mother and father, perhaps growing up without the gospel, there is no way to avoid the
heartache. Sin always brings misery, for the sinner and for
others involved. And when there has been a remarriage—
even in the rare occurrence when the remarriage has been
contracted biblically[1]—the stresses of the former marriage
continue to have impact on the new marriage as well. The
counselor should, therefore, probe for them when dealing
with divorces.

The typical strain of not seeing one's children except at
stated times, the possible conflict with the former spouse
over visits with the children, and the reactions of the new
spouse during visits from children are all areas for counseling exploration.

Where there has been a divorce and a remarriage, the
counselor first must be sure that any wrongs committed in
the transaction are righted before God and all parties involved. Nothing new and right can be built for the future
until the rubble of the past is cleared away. Secondly, the
counselor must help his counselees reach a joint biblical
stance toward the former spouse, the children, and their
visits. The believing couple must be willing to pray for the
salvation of the former spouse and children, and must
determine not to let their own heartache produce any added
strain on the children. It is absolutely necessary that they
talk out any current problems and keep communication
wide open for future discussions; only as they understand
and agree to a biblical stance will they be prepared to withstand even the severest future difficulty, which would otherwise drive a wedge between them.

The problems we have been considering will actually
strengthen the marriage of the husband and wife who face

1. Such occurrences are rare because the church usually has not made
sure that church discipline has been fully exercised and no sin remains
outstanding.

such challenges *together*. A genuinely unified stance can only accelerate growth in intimacy and trust. That is what the counselor aims for and sets before his counselees as a goal, which they can realize by facing their problems together God's way.

One factor that must be understood is that children living in another home are no longer under the authority of their former father or mother. The only influence a former authority may have upon them is now merely personal and exemplary. He or she, therefore, may neither purposely nor unwittingly undermine the new authority over the children. It is unfair to place children in a position where they are faced with what they perceive to be two conflicting authorities; they cannot serve two masters. If they are being injured, recourse can always be made to church discipline or, in the case of unbelievers, to the courts. But the counselee must not take it on himself to interfere with any reasonable discipline or authority.

In careful and judicious ways, the counselee must, however, continue to witness to unsaved children and seek the spiritual growth of saved ones. He may commit them to the Lord, and his new spouse should, together with him, take an interest in their spiritual welfare.

Business Influences

Another great outside influence is from social and business contacts connected with one's job. I speak of husbands, but with so many wives also employed, what I say applies as well to them.

Job influences are crucial simply because much of one's week is spent with business associates. That prolonged and regular contact may easily lead to dangerously close associations with evil companions. Unless, therefore, one draws clear limits to his associations and resolves not to transgress those limits, he will naturally drift toward companionships that could harm him and his marriage. Counselors must alert counselees to this fact.

A principal problem with work situations is that a person is thrown into constant contact with members of the opposite sex, many of whom make it a point to utilize business contacts for personal, social purposes. Unless a counselee is aware of this and is regularly on his (or her) guard, dangerous relationships may follow. The businessman, like the preacher, should heed Paul's advice: "Treat the younger women as sisters" (I Tim. 5:2). No sounder approach is possible.

Counselors should explore the possibilities of female attention at work that may undermine the marriage relationship; more often than counselors might think, that is at least part of the marital problem.

Social activities, like office parties, bowling teams, etc., should be carefully examined for any possible influence along this line. Strong ties with church activities and couples in the church should be cultivated instead, so that the counselee's close ties are among God's people. That might mean joining the church bowling league rather than the office league (even if it isn't as challenging), or some such change.

Some companies exert pressure on their employees, especially those who show potential for high management. The company may tell the person that if he wants to rise in the company he must put the company first, even before his wife and family. No Christian can submit to that advice. If he cannot persuade the company that he can do the job without sacrificing his biblical priorities, he may have to be content where he is or look for work in a company that doesn't make such requests.

Keeping Up with the Joneses

Several years ago I was shown the palatial mansion of the Joneses, of Jones and Laughlin Steel, located just outside of Pittsburgh. This is the home of the proverbial Joneses whom so many people try to keep up with, to the destruction of themselves and their marriages. Obviously, not many people succeed. But there are other "Joneses," closer to home and to our living standard, with whom we might try to keep up.

When we want too much, we often destroy our marriages in our attempts to get it. A counselor must carefully assess the desires (often erroneously called "needs") of his counselees. They may have to be told that their marriage would be much better off if they would forget about the Joneses, whether they are the Joneses of next door, or at work, or in TV ads.

This and the previous chapter have focused on the influence other personal contacts may have on a marriage. But such contacts are not the only personal influences a counselor need be aware of. There are also people we have never seen, and never will, who exert some of the strongest pressures on our marriages. We shall begin to consider these people and their influence in the next chapter.

Assignment

Draw up a plan you could present to a couple in which you detail the relationship they should sustain to one's children who live in a different home.

Hand in a paper discussing how parents may best tell their children that they will not have all of the toys or other supposed advantages the local "Joneses" lavish on their children. You are not talking about genuine gifts and advantages.

12

General Influences in Society

In considering those influences of which counselors should be well informed, it is important not to overlook the more general influences in society and culture. Though not as direct as a couple's own sinful patterns or misconceptions and the added influence of one's family or employment, the prevalent cultural milieu can exert an enormous pressure on marriages today.

Let me emphasize again, however, that culture in itself cannot influence a couple's marriage in a harmful way without their consent. Just as it is *how one responds* to the pressures of family and business associates, so too it is how one responds to cultural and social pressures that determines whether he is harmed or (where there is a fully biblical response) strengthened. The culture does not victimize him; he victimizes himself by yielding to the culture's temptations. It *is* possible to be "in the world but not of it." He therefore need not and must not subject his marriage to the evil influences of the culture around him.

Having reminded ourselves of that important principle, let us begin to discover what we can about some of our society's pervading influences that may lead to marriage difficulties.

Weakness of the Church

The church's weakness may not have occurred to you as a problematic cultural influence. There is a reason for that. The church is so weak, we don't even think of it as a cultural force; its impact on culture is almost nil. In the minds of many of its members, it does not provide a viable alternative to the influences of society. To that extent, it is part of the problem.

If we were to write a history of the church during the last two decades, we would have to note two significant trends: (1) the blessing of God in saving many people and multiplying the total resources of Bible-believing churches; (2) the proneness of the church to eclecticism in order to appear respectable in the eyes of the world.

The trend toward eclecticism shows up not only in counseling. You run into it everywhere: in the Christian school movement, in discussions of missionary strategy, in translation policies, in church management seminars—everywhere. In spite of the church's numbers and resources reaching an all-time high, she is weak because she has adopted many of the world's ideas, values, methods, practices, and "solutions" to problems. She has lost the cutting edge necessary to slice through the fabric of humanism and present a scriptural alternative. It has gotten so bad that in some circles the person who thinks and acts biblically is considered radical *within the church itself*.

The church must, therefore, shoulder some of the blame for the damaging influence of humanism on marriages. The greatest danger is that pagan products are being consumed from behind the label of Christian truth, and neither the peddlers nor the consumers seem to realize it. Though they mean well, they do great harm because the church has not adequately prepared its leadership or its members to discern carefully between good and evil.

Mobility, Anonymity

Ours has been called a "rootless society." The description is not inept. People move quickly, frequently, and over long distances, often into totally unknown communities. Christians are a part of this wandering tribe of Americans, who are constantly pulling up stakes and pitching their tents somewhere between Maine and California. In fact, many of them now travel and live abroad for long periods of time, as well.

In a rootless society the temptation is to become anonymous. The possibilities exist, as never before. And anonymous people face a great temptation to act irresponsibly. They have no one to encourage them to do good or to discourage them from evil. Yet all around them are the forces of evil trying to pull them down.

God never intended us to be lone-wolf, anonymous Christians. He made us to be parts of a community of faith where we might benefit from regular preaching and teaching of His Word, the godly encouragement of others, and the shepherdly oversight of elders, which would include the restoring balm of church discipline, if necessary. God knew that we would be aliens and strangers in this world, so He provided for that need. We cannot do without His provision.

There is, therefore, no excuse for Christian couples to become caught up in the world's influences when they may find encouragement and help almost anywhere they move. The Christian has a great advantage over others. He doesn't have to think of ways to meet the right people when he moves to a new community; as a child of God he has family all over. Immediately, he can find himself at home in a church of the Lord Jesus. The pagan, Caecilius Minocius Felix, had this to say about Christians in the early days: "They love one another almost before they know one another." That is how it can and should be today for a rootless Christian. Rootlessness is not his problem; he is a citizen of heaven and his taproot is there.

Many a couple, however, do not avail themselves of that great advantage. Like Lot, they pitch their tent toward Sodom. They look for the well-watered plains of the Jordan. They want to be comfortable. Unwilling to turn their backs on lucrative offers of advancement and greater salaries, they move into Sodom without ever considering whether there is a truly Christian church in the vicinity. So they limp along in a liberal church or quit going altogether. Then, like Lot, they vex their souls day by day, and ultimately their marriage and family are broken when their world collapses.

No Christian should move into a new location without first being sure that there is a viable church for himself and his family in the area. The forces of the world are far too great to withstand alone; God knew this and provided His church for our need. We must not lightly dismiss this need and God's provision for it.

Frequently counselors find that behind a person's difficulties lies a history of his neglecting fellowship with God's people. It is true, as I have said, that the church herself is weak and often deals in the wrong products. But among almost any group of genuine believers there can be found discerning people who clearly wish to better their lives and strengthen their families. The couple who remove themselves from God's church miss the benefits of fellowship in such a group. That core group of devoted believers could, in time, do much to bring a new spirit and a new

direction to the entire body. There is, therefore, no excuse
for disappearing from the life of the church. A part of every
counselor's task is to see that married couples are in a
proper relationship to a truly Bible-believing congregation.

Media

If there is one pervasive influence in society that impinges
on every Christian, and with which he must constantly
struggle, it is the news and entertainment media. Everywhere he turns—on billboards, in magazines, on radio, on
TV, in the newspapers, in books—he is bombarded with
values, ideas, and lifestyles that are out of accord with the
Bible. There is no escape from this assault on his senses and
his soul.

A counselee needs to be made aware that a TV program,
for example, is more than a casual production: it is a slick
piece of propaganda asserting a viewpoint that must be
evaluated. A counselee must, in fact, evaluate everything
around him all of the time. That is a big job. It doesn't allow
him to relax and go with the flow, as others do. He has to be
always at it—even in church, to be sure that the Sunday
school teacher isn't misrepresenting Scripture. The alert
Christian is the only one who can avoid the constant erosion
of his convictions under the relentless current of enemy
propaganda. One of the counselor's tasks is to make sure
counselees are alert to such matters.[1]

Most couples are not very alert. They soak up what the
world has to offer. Some of the worst of these offerings are
aimed at homemakers through women's magazines, which
have become vehicles for avant-garde thinking, and through
the daily TV soaps. To think that these soaps have no
impact on the thinking and living of those who watch them

---

1. The phrase "watch and pray" literally means "stay alert and pray."

day after day is but an idle dream. One pastor recently told me that at his weekly prayer meeting a woman requested prayer for a family in crisis. After she had described a few details of the crisis situation, another woman broke in, "Why that's the family on [such and such a TV soap]!" And it was. Here was a woman so caught up in the ongoing drama of this TV family that she actually confused it with a real need for prayer. And note, at least one other woman in the prayer meeting was familiar enough with the program that she could identify the fictitious drama.

Although we cannot totally avoid the onslaught of media propaganda, we can do two things: (1) reduce our contacts with it by cutting out objectionable TV programs, books, and movies, which glorify sin; and (2) become alert to and constantly evaluate whatever influences we cannot turn off.[2]

I do not need to go into detail, do I, about the emphases we find in the media? There is the glorification of illegitimate sex and of violence, the subtle downgrading of the church in which Christians, especially Christian ministers, are portrayed as nincompoops, the even more subtle acceptance of non-Christian values exemplified in the lives of TV heros, and so on.

Counselors must discover how much a married couple's values have been influenced by the media. Have they opted for abortion as an acceptable response to an unplanned pregnancy because of the insidious rhetoric of pro-abortionists?[3] Have they accepted the ideas of the feminist movement about building separate and equal careers or each marriage partner's becoming a person in his or her

2. The counselor must be prepared to help couples evaluate the effects of the milieu on them and their marriages; he should also be ready to suggest alternative lifestyles to replace sinful ones.

3. For example, references to unborn human life as "the product of conceptus," "a mass of cells," or "protoplasmic tissue," and the insistence that no limits should be placed on one's "right to choose."

own right? How, if at all, do such influences impinge on the marriage, and what has their effect been? Appropriate inquiry about such matters might prove very helpful in counseling. The counselor, upon discovering the extent of general media influence, may find it necessary to teach at length anti-cultural values from the Scriptures, thereby alerting the couple to what they have been soaking up by osmosis. He may find it necessary to urge them to abandon certain TV viewing, while substituting Bible study or a Christian reading program for it. In most cases, he must teach them how to become alert and how to evaluate what they see and hear around them, especially in advertising appeals.

Certainly, even the news media must be critically evaluated. Otherwise, subtle ideas and values that are a part of a reporter's pagan viewpoint will have their effect. What I am saying, in short, is this: There is enormous influence exerted all of the time by the media. It would be foolish for a counselor to ignore that fact.

Education

Little need be said here in addition to what I have said about media, because the same applies to what we learn from the schools. But this much must be added: We have been taught (even in Christian schools, inadvertently) that God isn't really a vital part of life; we can manage without Him most of the time. Consequently, God becomes a two-or-three-hour-a-week concern!

There is much wrong with education, including so-called "Christian" education—too much to detail in this limited space. In *Back to the Blackboard* I have examined the inroads of humanism in Christian education and proposed a truly

Christian alternative.[4] I cannot repeat what I have said there. Just let me say that the major problem with Christian schools is that they try to Christianize the pagan model down the street. You cannot Christianize what is essentially antithetical to all that is biblical. Because the Christian schools have tried, their students still emerge with the idea that Christianity is a one-day-a-week affair, that doctrine and life are unrelated, that the intellect is to be idolized above all else, that grades are the goal of life, and that education is for one's own advancement rather than for a life of love and ministry.

Those common examples of the world's ideas permeate the thinking and the lives of young couples whether they come out of Christian schools or public schools. Their training in humanistic values and practices for 12 plus years surely has its impact. Again, much anti-cultural instruction is needed to combat the baneful effects of this sort of education.

With so many influences bearing upon marriages, the wonder is that they are able to survive at all. Certainly the marriage counselor today has no easy task. Yet, this is a day of opportunity. The lines are being drawn more and more clearly by those who take these questions seriously and instruct their counselees accordingly. Surely, the least a counselor can do is alert his counselees to the effects of these forces and teach them how to withstand them.

4. Phillipsburg, N.J.: Presbyterian and Reformed, 1982.

Assignment

Be prepared to discuss ways to make the church aware of how it may be influenced by pagan values from the culture.

Draw up a teaching plan for instructing counselees about how to evaluate critically any influences of culture that may negatively influence their marriages. Include in the plan ways and means for withstanding these influences.

13

How to Discover
Marriage Problems

Asking Counselees Questions

I have emphasized, all along, the need for inquiring about problems and their causes. That means gathering data by asking counselees questions. Although various textbooks on counseling suggest otherwise, simple question asking remains the best method for finding out what a person's problems may be. So, let me say it plainly: If you want to gather facts about marriage problems, ask counselees to describe them.

Now, of course, not all counselees know what their problems are. So if you merely ask, "What are your problems?," you may not get all the information you need. That is why I have spent much time giving you a survey of the principal causes of marital difficulty—so that when you need more data, you can ask specifically, "What about the influence of relatives?" or "How about influences at work?" and so on.

While question asking is the one indispensable means of securing data on marriage problems, other methods are to be used in conjunction with it, though never in place of it.

Before turning to these other methods, let me emphasize
again—though I have said much about it in other books—
that it is vital to counsel husbands and wives *together*. Not
only does the Bible forbid gossip or talking negatively about
others behind their backs, which one-to-one counseling
often permits, but the counselor cannot get a true and full
picture from one highly emotional person without the other
there to correct what is said or supply missing information.
Proverbs 18:17 warns us:

> He who states his case first seems right until another
> comes to examine him.

A more powerful incentive for having both parties present
when gathering data could hardly be imagined.

I should also point out, before we look at other ways to
discover problems, that thorough data gathering is needed
to unearth problems more basic than the one for which a
couple come for counsel. For example, a couple may seek
help in disciplining their child. They have rightly presented
that as a problem area. But there may also be a problem in
their marriage, as there often is when child discipline is an
unresolved issue. It's not unusual for one spouse or both to
hope secretly that the marriage problem will emerge in the
course of counseling. And they may even say so after it has
come to light. Yet, because they are afraid to mention the
matter, it's up to the counselor to explore the possibility of
such a marital problem, especially in cases where children
are the focus. Not that a counselor should create deeper
problems where there are none; but he must be able to
detect the ones that do lie below the surface. And that calls
for thorough data gathering.

Other Ways to Gather Data

Closely allied to simple question asking is *having coun-*

selees write out everything that may be troubling their marriage.
This method differs from asking questions in the counseling session, where counselees must come up with answers
on the spot. Away from the emotionally charged counseling context, a person may calmly and methodically, over
the course of a week, write down all the factors that contribute to failure in his marriage. That is likely to produce a
fuller and more balanced response.

Data gathering through written assignments is a wise
step when you are not sure you have all the facts you need,
or you've had to use up much of the counseling session in
the important task of giving counselees hope.

*The ways a husband and wife speak to one another in the
counseling session* also reveals a lot about their marriage. As a
rule of thumb, I mentally exaggerate by tenfold any harsh
remarks and belligerent tones of voice, to get a rough idea of
what it must be like without the restraining presence of a
third party. Though only a rough estimate, that method
has checked out with counselees again and again as fairly
accurate.

In particular, listen to the *tone of voice*. Even endearing
terms like "Yes, dear" can be said scathingly. On paper,
those words look gentle and kind, but spoken in a cutting,
antagonistic tone, they can be among the cruelest and most
bitter of all.

Along the same lines, watch out for what Paul calls *"rotten" words*. They are not so much what we call "foul language," but words by which one person dices and cubes
another. Says Paul,

> Don't let a single rotten word come out of your mouths,
> but rather, whatever is good for constructively meeting
> problems that arise, so that your words may help those
> that hear (Eph. 4:29).

Unlike helpful words, which build up others, "rotten"

words (literally, *putrid* words) tear others down, leaving spoiled relationships. Sometimes these nasty words are couched in pointed "jokes" or asides. An alert counselor will watch for such words if he suspects marital problems. After three or more such expressions, he should ask if they are indicative of a problem in the marriage.

Some spouses become adept at *using a third party as a fulcrum*. With two partners deadlocked in contention, the counselor is viewed as a potential tie breaker, the pivotal vote in deciding who's right and who's wrong. Watch out for the temptation to take sides. It goes something like this: "Pastor, what do you think about . . . ?" The question sounds innocent enough to the unsuspecting pastor, and so he gives his opinion, upon which the one spouse exclaims, *"See* dear, he thinks so too!" Before he knows it, the pastor has been recruited to one side of the controversy.

If there is the slightest possibility of being used as a fulcrum whereby one spouse gets leverage against the other, the counselor should, at least temporarily, withhold his opinion. Better to inquire, "Why do you ask my opinion on that subject?"

Often a counselee's question is more slanted: "Don't you think such and such is true?" The question itself is a verbal crowbar soliciting your support. Instead of lending to the struggle, ask some questions of your own, as Christ often did. In Jesus' case it was not so much to gather data (He "knew what was in man") as it was to convict others about the intent of their loaded questions. For counselors today it serves both purposes.

Even if you are careful, you may find an adroit counselee enlisting your opinions to put pressure on another. All is not lost. You can redirect attention back to where it belongs: "Yes, that is my opinion, but my opinion is not half so important as what you did with it when you heard it. Look how you have used it against Helen! That's what we must talk about before we concern ourselves about the controversy itself." By putting the focus on the dynamic of (in this case) the husband's response, the counselor can show that there is more at stake than the question of who's opinion is correct.

Another way to detect problems in a marriage is by *recognizing radical changes*. Has the husband or wife recently become uncharacteristically careless or sloppy in appearance, manners, or actions? That may clearly signal marriage problems. One partner either is punishing the other or simply doesn't care any longer.

Some men or women do their utmost to "keep up a good front." They will go through all the outward amenities, often cooperating with each other in their efforts to hide their problem. With such couples you cannot rely on visible changes to indicate that there are problems. But when such changes do occur, they are strong evidence that something is wrong.

Indifference to a spouse's affection is also a reliable index. The indifference, or anger, is often one-sided. Not surprisingly, it may be greeted by *oversolicitousness*, as the unappreciated partner tries desperately to win back the other's affections. Efforts to do so can reach great lengths. Both the indifference and the excessive efforts reflect that the marriage is not as it should be.

Demanding the last word is another obvious indication that there is a problem. That is especially true when couples argue over little things that don't matter. Listen for ridiculous disputes, such as, "You are wrong. No such thing happened in the spring of '64, it was the winter." If it is important to distinguish whether something happened in the spring or in the winter, then of course that statement is no problem. But I am talking about making irrelevant details points of contention to be fought to the finish. Take note when someone *has to be right* all the time. The priorities in a marriage are out of line when one spouse or both insist on coming out on top.

Going along with the previous problem is *nagging and persistence*. The nag is someone who displays constant dissatisfaction with another for not doing something, or not doing it soon enough, or not doing it well enough. Persistence is an earmark of the nag. So watch for undue pertinacity on the part of one spouse or both. It spells trouble in a marriage.

Irritation is a sure sign of difficulty when it is constant. It is the flip side of nagging. Whereas nagging applies pressure, irritation reacts against it with sighs and groans, or verbal outbursts like, "I've had it up to here!" or "Sure, we're having trouble with the kids, but if she'd get off my back about disciplining them, it might just be possible for me to do so!"

As I said before, marriage is tested by problems. How well do marriage partners weather financial strains or child discipline problems, and the like? Do they pull together under pressure or start blaming one another? Ask yourself that sort of question when trying to determine whether there is a marriage problem. Look for the grosser responses to these questions. All marriages have their problems from time to time. What you want to know is whether they are overcome according to God's Word or they persist and lead to deepening problems. Any sinner can become irritated from time to time with his spouse. That is not the question. Is the irritation cleared up in a biblical way or not?—that is the real issue. So don't look for the occasional slip-up; look for the regular pattern. When you detect crowbar tactics, nagging, arguing over minute, insignificant matters, and so on, ask, "Is this part of a pattern? Does it happen often? Regularly?" That is what you are looking for.

You do not want to manufacture problems where they don't exist. That is why you must distinguish between occasional problems in a marriage, which are being dealt with biblically by confession and forgiveness, and the regular, ongoing ones, which are not.

Other Questions to Bear in Mind

To help you to discover marriage problems, consider also the following questions:

Is the couple unable to solve simple problems? When there are unresolved fights over toothpaste tubes—whether they should be squeezed in the middle or rolled up from the bottom, for instance—you know there is more to it than that. In such a case, the relationship is so sour that spouses are not willing to settle the simplest issue reasonably. Since the toothpaste tube is incidental—they could do battle over anything—it is fruitless to try to resolve that conflict until first their relationship has improved. The couple might focus on the point of contention, but you must table that issue until the contentiousness itself is cleared up in a biblical fashion. People who are at each others' throats will not resolve even small problems God's way. That is why you must first call for repentance and reconciliation.

Are there problems in a couple's sexual relationship? Usually sexual relationships go bad because of other problems, not because of anything directly connected with sex itself. What happens in bed at night reflects what has happened throughout the entire day. You can't carry a day's worth of unresolved problems into bed at night and expect to have a great time. So, if a couple complains of sexual difficulties, the solution almost always is reached by dealing with the other problems. In those infrequent cases where there is a physiological problem or where instruction in technique is necessary, the problem usually can be solved quickly. But such cases are rare. Look for problems elsewhere; that is where you can usually be most helpful.

Do the marriage partners have unrelated schedules? If the schedules of a husband and a wife barely overlap, you may suspect that either (1) they have arranged their lives to avoid contact and conflict with each other because of an unresolved problem, or (2) they have unwisely taken on too many obligations—a condition that, if continued, will lead to problems. Either way, schedules that allow a couple very little time together are a signal for marriage counseling.

Isolation can occur even when both parties are home—he in the basement workshop, and she in the sewing room. Or they may bury themselves in reading or TV and be worlds apart (although separate-but-parallel activities such as reading can provide a genuine sense of closeness). Repentance, followed by better planning and scheduling, is essential in all such cases.

A good question to interpose during counseling is, *Are there any matters you should have discussed with your spouse but have not?* If there are, the reason usually is fear, bitterness, anger, or just plain inconsiderateness. Whatever the reason, withholding important information or concerns will lead to difficulties in the home (cf. Eph. 4:25).

Another question that you may find productive is this: *Has there been growth, decline, or a plateauing of your marriage relationship during the last six months?* Obviously, the response can be of great significance, especially if the parties disagree. An answer of "growth" from one spouse and "decline" from the other points, at the very least, to a significant communication loss between them.

Since it is important to discover early that a marriage is on the skids, pastors and other counselors must urge couples to come for help without delay. The urgency of marriage counseling should be expressed in words like these: "Let me know when there is a problem you are unable to resolve yourselves. Don't wait until matters have deteriorated so

badly that you become severely antagonistic to one another. As soon as you discover you are in the quicksand and
unable to get out, shout for help. Yell loudly when the sand
is up to your ankles; don't wait until all I can get hold of is an
ear; it's a lot harder for everyone at that point!''

Assignment

In conjunction with others in the class, prepare a role play
of one of the cases in *The Christian Counselor's Casebook*,[1]
demonstrating how the counselor may use principles or
practices mentioned in this chapter to discover that a marriage is in trouble.

1. Phillipsburg, N.J.: Presbyterian and Reformed, 1974.

14
Illusions and False Solutions

There are many illusions about marriage problems and their solutions. A counselor should be familiar with them, not only to avoid them himself, but also to recognize them in his counselees' thinking. Some such illusions are the counselees' own misconceptions. Others come from well-meaning friends who do not understand either biblical principles of marriage or biblical practices of reconciliation. Clearing away illusory analyses of problems and false solutions is a major part of the counselor's task. He will therefore need both to understand them and to be able to show why they must be abandoned.

Perhaps the most common illusion is the notion that a marriage on the rocks can be *"patched up."* Such talk reflects meager expectations on the part of counselees. They hope for too little and are willing to settle for less than the biblical solution to their problem. The same attitude is behind such comments as, "We'll just have to make the best of a bad situation," or "If only you could get us back to where we were before this problem, though things weren't all that great then either."

In sharp contrast, the Christian approach is to solve all problems, not just solve some problems or solve them part way. Romans 5:20 tells us about the fullness of God's grace:

But where sin abounded, grace far more abounded.

That assurance means that when Christ meets sin, He more than meets the need. It is not His concern to "patch things up" or even to turn back the clock. He wants to turn a bad thing into a great one! And He will settle for nothing less.

The Christian counselor must not settle for anything less either. He wants to see problems solved and marriages brought to a better-than-ever condition. With Christ, his concern is to transform a bad marriage into a marriage that sings.

Bear in mind that salvation does not merely erase sin. Christ went beyond redeeming (buying back) what Adam lost. He brought man into a greater position than ever before—even in the garden. Man had been created a little lower than the angels, and when he sinned, he fell even lower. But in Christ's ascension and session at the right hand of the Father, He raised humanity far above the angels to the very throne of God Himself. That, as I said in a book by that name, is *more than redemption;* it is super-redemption!

Where sin abounds in a marriage, the grace of God can transform that marriage so that, in the end, grace is greater than all of the sin. God revels in using the very problems that He solves as a means for helping His children rise to greater heights than ever before. Counselors, therefore, should not allow counselees to set their sights on anything less. Low goals mean little progress. God makes even the wrath of man to praise Him.

A second illusion that must be countered is the attitude that a marriage is *"too far gone to change."* If there was little hope in the previous attitude, here there is none. So, why do people who are convinced their marriage is beyond hope come for counseling? To learn how to endure it or to end it with as little mess as possible. The Christian counselor will not settle for either of these nonsolutions. He will say instead, "No, that is not an option allowed by God. You have one option only: to change in God's way and by His power. The counselor will assure his listeners that change is possible, and he may even point to some biblical passages on which that hope is based. I will not mention all of them; each counselor is familiar with the ones he likes to use. But let me point out one that offers great hope for those involved in the most heinous sins. I Corinthians 6:9-11 deals with gross patterns of life. And yet Paul says of those who practiced the very same sins,

> these are what some of you were. But you were washed, you were sanctified, you were justified in the name of the Lord Jesus Christ and by the Spirit of our God (v. 11).

In that verse lies hope abounding. In spite of what one is involved in, whether homosexuality, adultery, greed, theft, or drunkenness (all matters thought by some to make marriage counseling hopeless), God says a person can put it behind him—just as the Corinthians did ("these are what you *were*"). In that great declaration lies hope for nearly every marriage problem.

A third problem encountered is stated this way: *"But I simply don't have any feeling for him/her anymore."* In this protest are two false assumptions. The first is that good feelings are necessary for loving another, and the second is that nothing can be done about the situation. Both assumptions are utterly false.

Let's consider the matter in regard to a husband who has repented of adultery. He truly wants things to be different in the future. But he admits, "I still have warm feelings for

the other woman and at best I have none for my wife."
What can you do for him?

The first thing he must be told is, "You are still making
investments in the wrong bank. Where your treasure is,
there your heart will be also. *Heart* means your whole inner
person, including your interests and your feelings." He
may not understand, and so you will have to push the
point: "Do you still have a picture of the other woman?"

"Well . . . yes."

"O.K., let me have it."

"What are you going to do with it?"

"Obviously, I'm going to tear it up and throw the pieces
into my trash can. If you are genuinely repentant, you will
do works appropriate to repentance. Here's a good place to
begin. Do you still have a key to her apartment?"

"Yes."

"Well, let me have that too. I'll put it into this envelope
and seal it. Now, you address it to the other woman. Good.
Now I'm going to give it to your wife to mail."

"Is there anything else, something you possess or do,
that is keeping your feeling alive? Do you pass her house on
the way to work? Do you. . . ." And so it must go. All the
investments he is still making in the wrong bank must be
stopped, and the account must be closed out.

On the other hand, according to the put-off, put-on principle, he must also begin to make heavy investments in his
wife. That means giving of his time, energy, and attention.
When he does freely and consistently, he will find that
before long his feelings have shifted.

Another illusion is expressed when one counselee or both
claim that a problem *"is not all that serious."* That is known in
biblical counseling circles as *minimizing the problem*. Rather
than minimize problems, biblical counselors note sadly,
with Paul, that "sin abounds." But with him they also
gladly affirm, "grace far more abounds."

Sometimes problem minimizers say, "All we need is a vacation." The helpful counselor responds, "I don't doubt that you may need a vacation, but a vacation will not solve your problem. Let's get the problem solved first; then you can enjoy the vacation!" Problems must be faced, not avoided. When the vacationer tries to avoid his problems, he either takes them with him or meets them on his doorstep when he returns home. That is no way to deal with problems. They must be recognized for what they are: sin. Sin is always serious and must be dealt with in a biblical fashion. Repentance, reconciliation, and the building of a new relationship to God and each other is what is needed, not a change of scenery.

Another evasion counselors hear often is that a problem *"will go away in time."* That view proposes to solve problems by *ignoring* them. Rarely, however, do problems just go away, even those not of our own sinful making. To think that they do is an illusion; it is hoping against hope, whistling in the dark. Spurgeon was on target when he said, "It is easier to crush the egg than to kill the serpent." Ignoring problems allows them to grow. You can ignore them for only so long before they reach grand proportions. Far better to face them biblically as soon as they are detected.

Even more illusory than the previous example is the line of thought that says a problem *"isn't really there."* As if to say, "What problem?," this self-deluding approach denies that something is obviously wrong in the marriage. I have actually heard the following conversation in a counseling session:

Wife: "Our marriage is falling apart."

Husband: "There isn't really any problem at all. She exaggerates everything."

What does the counselor do when he is faced with such an impasse? He says something like this: "Well, I don't yet know much about the problem in question, but I do know you have at least one serious problem."

Husband and wife: "What is that?"

"Simply this: If you can't agree on so important an issue as whether your marriage is falling apart, you have one whale of a communication problem. We'll start with that."

Finally, a seriously mistaken modern "solution" to marriage problems, which actually proposes sin, is the following: *"We have decided to separate for a time to think things through."* This miserable suggestion almost always shatters genuine hope by offering a false sense of peace in an escape from marriage problems. It furthermore violates I Corinthians 7:5, which is sin, and creates a temptation for each separating party.

Separation doesn't work. Counselors who foolishly advise such action learn the hard way that you simply can't put two people together by tearing them apart. The two must work together to solve their problems God's way, but they cannot do that if they are allowed to separate. As I have shown in my book *Marriage, Divorce and Remarriage in the Bible*, whenever the biblical word for *separate* occurs with reference to married persons, it means separation by *divorce*. The modern concept of legal separation was unknown in Bible times; and, as we have already seen, separation, legal or otherwise, was forbidden.

I have quickly run through several of the principal illusions and false solutions that counselors encounter all the time. Become aware of them, and be ready to respond to each. You will likely encounter one or more in your next two counseling cases.

Assignment

As a class, practice dealing with these objections and false solutions. Role play husbands and wives saying such things and counselors responding to them. Perhaps in this class endeavor you will discover additional ways of responding, which may prove useful in the days to come.

15

Basic Aims in Marriage Counseling

This very brief chapter, in effect, summarizes the most fundamental things I have said up to this point. By bringing all the basics together in one place, I hope to provide a statement of the whole picture that will remind you of the aims and goals to be borne in mind at all times in marriage counseling. Let me summarize in this way:

The basic aims in marriage counseling are

1. To secure a commitment from both parties to Christ and to His Word as the standard for all that is done and said,

which will

2. Foster and establish companionship between them, understood to be the essence of marriage,

leading to

3. Unity in intimacy,

which exhibits

4. Growth,

and which

5. Exemplifies the relationship between Christ and His church.

Though this statement is brief, it is comprehensive. The counselor who memorizes it and brings it to mind during all marriage counseling will find it helpful in holding him firmly to the fundamental course we have seen in the Scriptures.

Assignment

Discuss all of the various elements in the statement above in a comprehensive paper designed to amplify each point and demonstrate how it arises from biblical concerns. If you find it insufficient or in error at any point, discuss that too. The author would be happy to receive suggestions growing out of a class concensus.

16

Problems Peculiar to Sex Roles: Part One, Wives

Of the many issues that could be raised in this chapter, I shall confine myself to three: submissive help, relationships to children, and biological change.

Submissive Help

The word *submission* comes up frequently in discussion of a wife's role in marriage because of its use in Ephesians 5 and I Peter 3. And it should. Those passages clearly urge wives to "submit" to their husbands. But as is often the case, the term is currently used without adequate regard for its biblical definition.

In order to explain submission in a biblical way, let's first look at the two principal passages mentioned above:

> Wives, submit yourselves to your own husbands as to the Lord, since a husband is the head of his wife as Christ is the Head of the church; He Himself is Savior of the body. But as the church is subject to Christ, so also should wives be to their husbands in everything.

. . . and the wife must respect her husband (Eph. 5:22-24, 33b).

In the same way, wives, submit yourselves to your own husbands, so that even if some of them disobey the Word they may be won without a word through the behavior of their wives, by observing your respectful, pure behavior. Your adornment must consist not of outward things such as the braiding of hair, and putting on of gold jewelry or clothing yourselves with robes; rather, beautify the hidden person of the heart with the incorruptible quality of a gentle and quiet spirit, which is of great value before God. Indeed, in this way also holy women of the past who put their hope in God beautified themselves, submitting to their own husbands, as, for example, when Sarah obeyed Abraham, calling him lord. And you will have become her children by doing good and fearing no intimidation (I Pet. 3:1-6).

These two classic passages have all the essentials on the submission of wives to their husbands. Looking closely at both, you will find that submission consists of two things: *respect* and *obedience*.

Since few people analyze submission in a biblical fashion, it may do no good for a counselor merely to order a wife to submit to her husband. Her first problem is that she does not know what "submit" means. You must be able to explain it to her. Moreover, you must be able to answer objections and clear up misunderstandings. Otherwise, you will either get no compliance, or unwittingly encourage a strange and twisted compliance to some extrabiblical idea, instead of biblical submission.

Respect

"How can I respect a man who lies around in the gutter

drunk?," asks one wife. Another objects, "Yes, or a man who beats his children and ignores his wife?" These are valid and important questions for the Christian marriage counselor. How does a wife respect an unsaved, sinfully living husband? After all, Peter expects wives to submit to unbelieving husbands, "even if some of them *disobey* the Word." How does a wife do that?

A Christian wife can respect even an uncouth, unbelieving husband, not for what he is *in himself*, but for his authoritative role.

When a traffic officer stops you for speeding, you do not insist, "Just a minute, officer. I need to know some facts about your personal background before I agree to accept this ticket." You know better than to try that. His authority to direct traffic and to ticket you does not stem from his personal beliefs, character, or actions. It issues from the government he represents. You submit to him because God tells you to submit to all governing authorities.

The same is true of Christian wives: They are to submit to their husbands, not because of any supposed authority residing in those men, but because of the authoritative capacity in which God places husbands as the heads of their homes. That is not an internal, inherent authority (*dunamis*) but an externally conferred authority (*exousia*). And since a husband's authority is conferred on him by God, it is God whom wives respect when they respect their husbands, and it is God whom they disrespect when they don't.

These points must be made clear to women who object to respecting their husbands. A wife's speech and attitudes in reference to her husband should be predicated on her respect for God and His conferred authority. That is why Peter urges wives to maintain "a gentle, quiet spirit . . . before God." As the army says, "Salute the uniform, not the man."

Obedience

"Respect I can see, but obedience—that is another matter," says one wife who doesn't like to "take orders from" her husband. What about this matter of obedience? As Peter makes abundantly plain, it too is a part of submission: "as, for example, when Sarah *obeyed* Abraham, calling him lord."

Is a wife to obey her husband in all things? Yes, according to Ephesians 5:24. This means, of course, in all things over which God has granted husbands authority. God's authority given to the church, to business, to the state, and to the home is, in each case, a *limited* authority. It extends only to those areas within the purview of the authority granted. To the church alone has been given the authority to preach the Word; that is not the function of the state. When the state forbade the church to preach in Christ's name, the apostles replied, "We must obey God rather than men." Their choice was not between two equally valid, though contradictory, authority-commands of God. No, clearly they considered the state to have exceeded its authority-grant from God when they described its authority as purely human: ". . . rather than *men*." Likewise, to the state alone is given the power of the sword (Rom. 13); it would be entirely wrong, therefore, for the church or the home to take up the sword. Even if a person clearly deserves the death penalty, a husband obviously has no right to ask his wife to carry it out. That prerogative belongs to the state. God never granted it to the home. A wife, therefore, is to obey her husband in everything under his legitimate authority, but *not without limits*. The realm of authority is bounded by the Scriptures.

Scripture also limits a husband's authority in that God never authorizes sin. The idea that wives must obey their husbands even when commanded to sin is foreign to the

Bible. If, then, a husband commands his wife to accompany him on a weekend of spouse-swapping, she must respectfully refuse, saying, "Please don't ask me to sin; I may not. God commands me not to commit adultery. He did not give you the right to command it." Notice, a wife is to emulate Sarah in "doing good and fearing no intimidation," not in cooperating with evil. A wife ought not succumb to pressure to do wrong or fear the consequences of standing for what is right. The call for her not to fear intimidation shows that a wife's godly submission is not always the path of least resistance.

Of course, most problems related to a wife's submission do not have to do with these limitations on the husband's authority. They usually center on conflicts over matters of expedience or preference entirely within the husband's right to command. Here she must be willing to obey—even when she doesn't like it. If there is any question, she should give her husband the benefit of the doubt and obey.

Keeping these parameters clearly in mind is important when counseling wives who have trouble with submission. There is, of course, more that could be said about submission, which I will address in the following chapter on husbands as heads, and in the next section on wives as helpers.

The Helping Wife

A wife is not a *slave*. Far from it. The ideal woman set forth in Proverbs 31 was an exciting, well-rounded person who was "with it" intellectually and in every other way.[1] As we have seen, a wife's submission is not passive, blind obedience. It is thoughtful, helpful input into the working order

1. For more on Proverbs 31, see my exposition of the passage in *Christian Living in the Home*.

of the home. She should offer such input freely and respectfully, and her husband should give it full and careful consideration. She is his helpful companion. Genesis 2:18 is
explicit:

I will make him a helper who is appropriate to him.

As the answer to man's loneliness, a wife is a companion
in the fullest sense—she is a "helper." Notice, that help is
not confined to cooking her husband's meals and washing
his clothes. The text places no limitations on the kind of help
she affords. She is to be his helper *in all things*. Her help is an
essential element in her companionship. We might para-
phrase the first part of Genesis 2:18 to read, "It is not good
for the husband to make decisions alone." The central characteristic of the model wife in Proverbs 31 is that she helped
her husband at all points. Because she did, her husband
rose to a place of leadership as an elder sitting in the city hall
(the "gates").

That means that if a husband's thinking is out of line, his
wife's task is to help him correct his thoughts. If his life is
out of line, her job is to help him return to God's path. If he
simply is perplexed in a decision, she must bring her best
reasons to the decision-making process. Help, given respectfully, never conflicts with submission. That is because
submission requires her *to contribute,* to give what she has to
offer. And that is what she must do, always in a spirit of
respect and with a willingness to obey even if she may not
agree. As a body with more than one head is a monstrosity,
so too, there must be only one head to a home.

Since the wife's role as helpful companion applies to all
matters in the home, failures in that connection can produce
raging conflicts at any number of points in the marriage.
You can imagine what happens when, instead of being in
her husband's corner, pulling for him, assisting him in his
life work, giving him ideas, working for the same goals as

he, a wife does just the opposite. There is no shortage of wives who, in disgust with their husbands, do all they can to be a hindrance. The wife crosses her husband's efforts in child discipline, sabotages his plans, refuses to offer suggestions, then criticizes when things go wrong. Rather than pull *for* him, she turns the marriage into a tug of war.

A husband can have no greater help or hindrance than what his wife gives him. Since opposing God's authority is the essence of sin, marriage counselors should be on the lookout for ways in which wives oppose the God-ordained leadership of husbands. Pointing out such hindrances, counselors need to call for repentance and then train wives to become helpers. It is not enough to get them to confess their sins of not being helpful companions; they must be trained to "put on" helpful deeds, a step many counselors overlook.

Children

Here I want to emphasize what I mentioned briefly before, that when a wife grows lax in her relationship to her husband, she tends to focus attention that should be directed toward him, onto her children—especially her boys. Because women are person-oriented, and wives generally spend more time with children than do husbands, it is not surprising that if she misdirects her interests, they usually settle on her children. Whenever a wife substitutes a child for her husband as the object of her helpful companionship, the relationship to her husband further deteriorates. Sooner or later the relationship with that child will deteriorate too. When the time comes for him to leave home and perhaps marry, his mother will tend to hold on to him or cause trouble over the marriage. Moreover, when the break does come, she will not automatically return her affections to her husband. A difficult readjustment will lie ahead, especially if that is the last child, and the only one left is her husband.

So much more could and should be written on this area that a book on *The Christian Mother and Her Children* is long overdue. Our present, specific concern is to alert counselors to this tendency among wives and the need for repentance, as well as instruction in how wives can refocus energies and affections back onto their husbands, as God requires.

Biological Changes

A reminder to counselors and husbands is in order, that women do face monthly periods and changes of life. Because of the biological changes in hormones and other factors in these natural, but difficult, processes, women are faced with temptations men do not face. It is not that wives are forced into nastiness or depression by these changes, any more than someone else who suffers from some stressful bodily change that presents the temptation to be short with or withdraw from others. But the temptation is there. Counselors should encourage wives to tell husbands when they are undergoing premenstrual stress or hot flashes from changes of life, so that husbands can take these into consideration.[2]

Conclusion

Without discussing all the particular situations possible, I have set forth the essential principles regarding a wife's role

2. A pamphlet on this subject, which may be helpful as a handout for counselees, is available from The Christian Counseling and Educational Foundation, 1790 East Willow Grove Ave., Laverock, PA 19118.

in marriage. Counselors who gain a firm grasp of those principles can apply them to the particular cases that arise, whatever their peculiar features may be.

Assignment

Study the following questions. Be prepared to discuss them in class, giving biblical reasons for your conclusions:

1. An unsaved husband tells his wife that she is never to darken the door of the church again. How would you advise her?

2. A wife knows that her husband is making a wrong decision that could have disastrous effects on the future of the family. What would you tell her to do?

3. A husband refuses to allow his wife to make suggestions, even in a submissive manner. He says, "God made me the head of this home; your job isn't to offer your opinion, it is merely to obey." What would you do about this?

4. A husband refuses to assume leadership in the home and, because his wife is wise in making decisions, casts the entire responsibility on her. Would you advise her to accept it?

17

Problems Peculiar to Sex Roles: Part Two, Husbands

Having considered the wife first, as did Peter and Paul in the passages cited in the previous chapter, let me now set forth the pertinent texts on the role of husbands:

> Husbands, love your wives just as Christ loved the church and gave Himself up for her so that He might sanctify her, cleansing her by the washing of water with the Word, that He might present the church to Himself gloriously arrayed, not having spot or wrinkle or any such thing, but rather that she might be holy and without blemish. In the same way, husbands ought to love their wives as they love their own bodies. Whoever loves his wife loves himself. Nobody ever hated his own flesh, but rather nourishes and cherishes it just as Christ does for the church—we are members of His body. "For this reason a man shall leave his father and mother and shall cleave to his wife and the two shall be one flesh." There is a great secret in this, but I am speaking about Christ and about the church. Nevertheless, each one of you also must love his wife the same way that he loves himself (Eph 5:25-33).

And He has subjected everything under His feet, and made Him head over all things for the sake of the church (Eph. 1:22).

Husbands, likewise live with your wives in an understanding way, showing respect for the woman as you would for a fragile vase, and as joint heirs of the grace of life, so that your prayers may not be interrupted (I Pet. 3:7).

These are the three classical passages concerning the man's role in marriage. In them, you will discover that two elements predominate: loving leadership and gentleness.

Loving Leadership

Love

Nowhere in the New Testament is the wife commanded "love your husband."[1] But, in the space of the few verses in Ephesians 5, four times the husband is commanded to love his wife. Love clearly is the task of the husband and not the wife. The husband is to initiate love, to maintain love, and to see that love grows in the marriage. That is his responsibility.

Since not one in a hundred Christian husbands knows that fact, counselors must enlighten men as to their responsibility. When a husband complains that there is no love left in his marriage, the faithful counselor responds, "Well, sir, if that is true, the problem is primarily your fault." Too many husbands think that, like lifeboats, love is for women and children. They view it as a sticky, sentimental, effeminate predisposition. The counselor must show

---

1. Titus 2:4 is no exception; the word in the original means "be affectionate to": the "mature women" are to teach the younger women "to be affectionate to their husbands."

them otherwise. Love *gives* and, therefore, is as manly as Christ's giving of Himself on the cross.

Husbands can be expected to ask, "Why is love *my* responsibility?" The biblical counselor must be prepared to explain further, "Because the marriage relationship, says Paul, must reflect the love of Christ for His church." It was not the church that first loved Christ; He Himself took the initiative, so that while we were weak sinners, even enemies (there was nothing in us to commend us to Him), He set His love on us. As John put it in I John 4:19, "We love because [Christ] *first* loved us." Until husbands understand this fact and commit themselves to following it, they will never fulfill their roles as leaders in the home. It is not just leadership that they are to exercise, but *loving* leadership.

Since I have discussed love in depth elsewhere, I shall say no more about it here, except to emphasize its inseparable connection with headship.

Headship

A husband's headship is a loving headship, because it is like Christ's. It is not just any kind of headship. Although people have various ideas on this subject, the headship of Christ is the only biblical model. It is markedly different from that of rulers or business executives, for example. Christ's is a headship characterized by sacrificial love in which He gave Himself for the church, over which He is Head.

In Ephesians 1:22, Christ's headship is described as being *for the sake of the church*. If Christ's headship is for the sake of His bride, the church, and a husband's headship is to reflect that of Christ, then all that a husband does as head should be for the sake of his wife. All decisions are to be made with her best interests and welfare in mind. The headship of a well-informed, obedient Christian husband is something in which his wife should delight. Though his authority gives him the last word in responsible decision making, biblical headship requires him to put his wife first in all things, as Christ does the church.

Gentleness

Gentleness is an outstanding feature in the various passages on how a husband should treat his wife. Though I am not sure why that is, the reason may be a desire to upgrade the status of wives in the eyes of men who had been converted from paganism with all of its cruelty. One thing is certain; gentleness emerges as a significant factor in these biblical accounts. Paul, for example, uses two of the tenderest Greek words to describe the concern a husband must have for his wife. Those words, translated by two of the tenderest words in English, *nourish* and *cherish,* accord perfectly with the notion that he is to exercise a loving leadership over her, seeking her benefit and blessing.

The way to treat one's wife is the way you would handle a fragile vase—with the utmost care and concern. She is to be nourished and cherished as one nourishes and cherishes his own body. Clearly, there is no place for the feminist emphases here. While a husband and wife are equals in relation to God as heirs of the grace of eternal life, his is the protective, caring, concerned, and gentle role, which she is not told to exercise in relationship to him. He is not to submit to her, and she is not to be head over him. As she is to respect and obey him, he is gently to lead and love her.

A husband's loving leadership and gentleness in caring for his wife are ways in which he is to be Christ-like in the marriage relationship. As he studies the New Testament to learn of Christ's loving rule of His church, the Christian husband will discover in greater detail what God expects of him. Two books that will be found helpful in this regard are Wayne Mack's *How to Develop Deep Unity in the Marriage Relationship* (Phillipsburg, N.J.: Presbyterian and Reformed, 1977) and *A Homework Manual for Biblical Counseling*, vol. 2, *Family and Marital Problems* (Phillipsburg, N.J.: Presbyterian and Reformed, 1980).

Assignment

Write a comprehensive paper describing how a husband is to relate to his wife. The material in this paper should *not* be taken from the passages quoted in this chapter, but from other passages that describe how Christ heads up His church and what He does for her in love.

Conclusion

As counselors clearly explain marriage roles to husbands and wives, they will help them recognize harmful attitudes that are behind any number of marital problems. They will also train spouses in new, biblical attitudes and the actions that should accompany them.

It is of crucial importance that counselors not allow one spouse to use the failure of the other as an excuse for not doing what he or she should. Each partner is to mind his or her *own* responsibilities toward the other, not focus on the other's shortcomings. Obedience in marriage is, first of all, service to Christ and, second, for the sake of one's spouse. It is not for the purpose of evoking a desirable response from the other partner. This point needs to be uppermost in the marriage counselor's thinking.

Having become aware of the principal problems mentioned in this book—how to spot them and how to resolve them—you will develop skill for applying those insights only through their continued use in a variety of cases. To help you develop flexibility in applying biblical principles to the wide variety of situations you will face, I have written another volume entitled *Insight and Creativity in Christian Counseling*. That book will help you extend the implications and applications of this book to areas not spelled out here.

I would also suggest that you keep this book within reach for reference and review, so that as you encounter particular cases, you will be able to go back to the relevant sections with a more vibrant, personal concern than perhaps before.

May the great Husband of the church bless you as you minister in His name, that you might help many who have no idea of what is wrong with their marriages or what to do about it. May you help them not only to find God's solutions to their problems, but to grow in their relationship to Him and each other. Then they will truly exemplify the proper relationship of Christ to His church.

The Christian Counselor's Manual
The Practice of Nouthetic Counseling
Jay E. Adams

The Christian Counselor's Manual is a
companion and sequel volume to the author's
influential *Competent to Counsel*. It takes the
approach of nouthetic counseling introduced
in the earlier volume and applies it
to a wide range of issues, topics, and
techniques in counseling:

- Who is qualified to be a counselor?
- How can counselees change?
- How does the Holy Spirit work?
- What role does hope play?
- What is the function of language?
- How do we ask the right questions?
- What often lies behind depression?
- How do we deal with anger?
- What is schizophrenia?

These and hundreds more questions are answered in this
comprehensive resource for the Christian counselor. A full set
of indexes, a detailed table of contents, and a full complement
of diagrams and forms make this one of the best reference
books currently available for Christian counselors.

Jacketed Hardcover
ISBN: 0-310-51150-X

Pick up a copy today at your favorite bookstore!

ZONDERVAN™

GRAND RAPIDS, MICHIGAN 49530 USA

WWW.ZONDERVAN.COM

Competent to Counsel

Introduction to Nouthetic Counseling

Jay E. Adams

This is a classic in the field of Christian counseling. It has helped thousands of pastors, students, laypersons, and Christian counselors develop both a general approach to Christian counseling and a specific response to particular problems. Using biblically directed discussion, nouthetic counseling works by means of the Holy Spirit to bring about change in the personality and behavior of the counselee. As the author points out in his introduction, "I have been engrossed in the project of developing biblical counseling and have uncovered what I consider to be a number of important scriptural principles . . . There have been dramatic results . . . Not only have people's immediate problems been resolved, but there have also been solutions to all sorts of long-term problems as well." First published in 1970, this book has gone through over thirty printings. It establishes the basis for an introduction to an approach to counseling that is being used in pastors' studies, in counseling centers, and across dining room tables throughout the country and around the world.

Jacketed Hardcover
ISBN: 0-310-51140-2

Pick up a copy today at your favorite bookstore!

ZONDERVAN™

GRAND RAPIDS, MICHIGAN 49530 USA

WWW.ZONDERVAN.COM

The Handbook of Church Discipline
A Right and Privilege of Every Church Member
Jay E. Adams

This is a handbook for pastors, elders, and all
Christians who want to see how Scripture
presents the process of discipline that should
operate in the Christian community. It was
written in response to an urgent need. In
order to help church leaders deal with the
sorts of problems that require the church to
respond with discipline, the author has
developed the book around the five steps
of corrective discipline found especially in
Matthew 18:15–17. Because there is not
merely one kind or one stage of discipline, church leaders must
learn how to discern. And once the right discernment has been
made, then the right action can follow. This is a simple and very
readable little handbook. The influence it can and should have
on the church is, however, quite profound.

Softcover
ISBN: 0-310-51191-7

Pick up a copy today at your favorite bookstore!

ZONDERVAN™

GRAND RAPIDS, MICHIGAN 49530 USA

WWW.ZONDERVAN.COM

How to Help People Change
The Four-Step Biblical Process
Jay E. Adams

"While touching on many aspects of counseling, this book... is specifically designed to elucidate the process of counseling. I have often mentioned and illustrated that process, but not in the focused and systematic way that the four-step biblical process is set forth here... This book presents a fresh perspective not only on how to counsel, but also on what measures to take at what stages of counseling."
— *Jay Adams, from the Preface*

Change is the essential goal of the counseling process. And Christian counselors recognize, as the author is so concerned to remind us, "Substantial change requires the alteration of the heart." How does a Christian counselor work in order to bring about this kind of change? The answer is found, of course, in Scripture—in 2 Timothy 3:14—17, to be specific. Jay Adams is well known as a counselor who bases his whole approach to counseling on Scripture. This book offers the interested reader an unparalleled opportunity to see both how he discovers and applies biblical principles and the way in which Scripture functions as the basis of his approach to counseling. This book answers not only the question "How does a counselor help people change?" but also "How does Scripture operate as the source of a counselor's method?" It is a book that has much to say about the ongoing discussion of the relationship between theology and psychology in the enterprise of Christian counseling.

Softcover
ISBN: 0-310-51181-X

Pick up a copy today at your favorite bookstore!

ZONDERVAN™

GRAND RAPIDS, MICHIGAN 49530 USA

WWW.ZONDERVAN.COM

Marriage, Divorce, and Remarriage in the Bible
A Fresh Look at What Scripture Teaches Us
Jay E. Adams

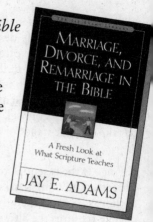

Marriage, Divorce, and Remarriage in the Bible is a book that many pastors, counselors, and theologians consider to be the most biblical and the most helpful on the issue of marriage and divorce. If the church is going to use the Bible to decide whether divorce is legitimate in certain cases and whether divorced people have the right to remarry with the approval and blessing of God's people, then the Bible must be studied without prejudice toward a particular answer. The book examines the relevant passages in both the Old and New Testaments so that readers can consider the many issues and interpretations that arise in trying to establish a consistently biblical position. As a result, readers can see more clearly and accept more firmly the truth of Scripture.

Softcover
ISBN: 0-310-51111-9

Pick up a copy today at your favorite bookstore!

ZONDERVAN™

GRAND RAPIDS, MICHIGAN 49530 USA

WWW.ZONDERVAN.COM

Preaching with Purpose
The Urgent Task of Homiletics

Jay E. Adams

"The amazing lack of concern for purpose among homileticians and preachers has spawned a brood of preachers who are dull, lifeless, abstract and impersonal; it has obscured truth, hindered joyous Christian living, destroyed dedication and initiative, and stifled service for Christ."
— *Jay Adams, from chapter 1*

Preaching needs to become purposeful, says Jay Adams, because purposeless preaching is deadly. This book was written to help ministers and students discover the purpose of preaching and the ways that the scriptures inform and direct the preaching task. *Preaching with Purpose*, like the many other books of Jay Adams, speaks clearly and forcefully to the issue. Having read this book, both students and experienced preachers will be unable to ignore the urgent task of purposeful preaching. And the people of God will be the better for it.

Softcover
ISBN: 0-310-51091-0

Pick up a copy today at your favorite bookstore!

ZONDERVAN™

GRAND RAPIDS, MICHIGAN 49530 USA

WWW.ZONDERVAN.COM

Shepherding God's Flock
A Handbook on Pastoral Ministry, Counseling, and Leadership
Jay E. Adams

Shepherding God's Flock is both a textbook for students of pastoral ministry and a handbook for pastors. In its three parts most of the tasks of pastoral ministry are outlined, and a practical approach to those tasks is developed. Jay Adams is well known for his practical and thorough approach to the many issues of Christian counseling. That same practicality and thoroughness is found in this unparalleled handbook on pastoral ministry. Not only does it offer pastors one of the best resources in print; it provides church elders orientation and practical guide to aspects of ministry for which they have responsibility. It is truly a shepherd's handbook. The book is divided into three parts: Pastoral Life deals with the pastor, his calling, and the general care he provides the flock. Pastoral Counseling provides an overview of the task and a general approach for pastoral counselors. Pastoral Leadership offers a perspective on the ways the pastor can lead the church in its many tasks and responsibilities.

Softcover
ISBN: 0-310-51071-6

Pick up a copy today at your favorite bookstore!

ZONDERVAN™

GRAND RAPIDS, MICHIGAN 49530 USA

WWW.ZONDERVAN.COM

A Theology of Christian Counseling
More Than Redemption
Jay E. Adams

A Theology of Christian Counseling is a book that connects biblical doctrine with practical living. Salvation, that central concern of Protestant theology, is often too narrowly defined. It is thought to be "being saved from the consequences of sin." But God is doing much more. He is making something new out of the old sinful nature. He is, in Christ, making new creatures. "No counseling system that is based on some other foundation can begin to offer what Christian counseling offers . . . No matter what the problem is, no matter how greatly sin has abounded, the Christian counselor's stance is struck by the far-more-abounding nature of the grace of Jesus Christ in redemption. What a difference this makes in counseling!" In this book the reader will gain an insight into the rich theological framework that supports and directs a biblical approach to counseling. And the connection between solid theology and practical application will become compelling. This is a one-of-a-kind. Don't ignore it!

Softcover
ISBN: 0-310-51101-1

Pick up a copy today at your favorite bookstore!

ZONDERVAN™

GRAND RAPIDS, MICHIGAN 49530 USA

WWW.ZONDERVAN.COM

We want to hear from you. Please send your comments about this
book to us in care of zreview@zondervan.com. Thank you.

GRAND RAPIDS, MICHIGAN 49530 USA

WWW.ZONDERVAN.COM